THREE CENTURIES OF BALLET

By the same Author:

DORIS NILES, AND A SUMMARY OF THE SPANISH DANCE

(Edited by Cyril W. Beaumont, London, 1937)

Library of Congress Catalog Card Number: 52-12854
PRINTED IN THE NETHERLANDS

CORNELIUS CONYN

THREE CENTURIES

of

BALLET

ELSEVIER PRESS, INC.
HOUSTON–NEW YORK
1953

INTRODUCTION

In the following chapters a short survey of the dance as an art is given, the author's aim being to whet the reader's appetite for insight and knowledge rather than to satisfy it.

The casual member of an audience, who has been emotionally stirred, or made happy and gay, by watching a dance performance, may want to know something more about the background of this varied art. He may rightly feel that some knowledge of its history, its technique, and its various mediums of artistic expression would help to make his appreciation the keener and his satisfaction the deeper.

Any approach to the stage dance in general has to deal with the growth of classical and modern ballet, as this is to date the most powerful and civilized expression of the dance as a cultural phenomenon. But other forms of dance expression have been described here also, however briefly. And although no more than a bird's-eye view of the whole field has been possible, it will enable the reader whose interest has been awakened in a particular aspect of the dance to find more detailed information in other publications. For the same reason the technique of ballet has been given merely in outline, with as little use of technical terms as possible. For instance, the true balletomane would use the international dance jargon with authority when witnessing a ballet, and might hold forth about the perfection of a *sissonne* or a *fouetté ronde de jambe en tournant*, which in plain English means a kind of turn in which the dancer, balancing on one toe, obtains propulsive power by lashing out her free leg to the side, and bending it in sharply from the knee as she revolves.

Such knowledge may be of interest, but it is not essential to the average spectator.

This book is for him, and not for the balletomane, who has had ample opportunity for observation and study. It is for those who are interested in the story of the development of various dance styles throughout the last three centuries, but who have not sufficient leisure to dedicate to the study of this particular art. If it may only serve as an introduction to the æsthetic joys of ballet and other dance styles, and point the way towards a more general appreciation and towards an understanding of the true importance of the dance in our cultural life, the authors' purpose will have been achieved.

One last remark: ballet history is a living thing. Some facts of the contemporary scene at the time of writing, have been altered at the time of printing in 1953. For instance the famous couples Markova and Dolin, and Fonteyn and Helpmann have split. Some companies mentioned will soon have to be referred to in the past tense. Facts presented roughly describe the dance world between 1600—1950.

ACKNOWLEDGMENTS

MY warmest thanks are due to the following artists, societies and private collectors, who kindly allowed me to reproduce much of the photographic material, which is such a valuable contribution to this book:

French Press Service in Australia, and Monsieur G. Leroy-Terquem
New Zealand Government Tourist Bureau
Portuguese Ministry of Information, Lisbon
Swiss Consulate of Sydney
U.K. Information Service
U.S. Information Service
John Lanting, Amsterdam
Ram Gopal, Bangalore
A. Nipius (Studio Rembrandt), Brisbane
Madame Hélène Kirsova, Copenhagen
L. M. G. Arntzenius, Madame Yvonne Georgi and Peter van Hoboken, the Hague
The Hon. Rhys Davies, London
Serge Leslie and Madame Doris Niles, Los Angeles
Pilar Lopez, Madrid
Martha Graham, S. Hurok, Inc., and G. Wilfred Neilson, New York
Madame Marie Colin, Comtesse de Cardon, and Dr. René Vaillant, Paris
Madame Gertrud Bodenwieser, Edouard Borovansky, William Constable, Dr. A. Fleischmann, Dr. A. Laborinho, Loudon Sainthill, Ure Smith Pty. Ltd., Mrs. Patricia Thompson, and the editors of 'Pix', Sydney.

Arnold L. Haskell, London, for his authorization to quote from his works
Miss Eleanor Fitzgerald Martin, Sydney, for the design of a ballet *décor* used for the endpapers
Jon Chisholm Marten, Sydney, for his valuable help in furnishing and checking data, and in correcting proofs.

CONTENTS

ILLUSTRATIONS

CHAPTER ONE

CULTURAL DEVELOPMENT OF THE DANCE

*Dancing consists in the rhythmical movement of any or all parts
of the body, in accordance with some scheme of individual or con-
certed action, which is expressive of emotions or ideas*

Encyclopaedia Britannica

ORIGIN

THE dance is one of the oldest emotional expressions known to mankind. Even the Australian aboriginals, who are among the most primitive tribes known in the world to-day, have their corroborees. These are less a studied art than a primitive form of self-expression and of animistic ritual, stylised through the convention of many generations into set figures of plastic movement, ceremonies and sequences.

The primary impulses which primitive peoples express in movement are joy, fear, the battle-urge and sex. We find the latter, one of the deepest urges, expressed even in the bird dances of the animal kingdom during mating season, with the preening and prancing of the male to dazzle the female. Compare these prancings with some of the folk dances, such as those of the Bavarian peasants, where one village beau tries to outdo the other in feats of rhythmic agility and jumping before a fair audience.

The oldest form of dancing must have been the virile demonstration of energy and skill given by the earliest men in search of their women. It survives to this day in tribal dances of various continents. The warrior-dances came next, their frenzy of movement and the accompanying chants or shouts lashing the opponents into a fury. Similar dances, performed to placate the wrath of unseen spirits, embodying the age-old elements of superstitious fear, often ended in the supreme sacrifice of human victims. In a higher form, with a slightly more advanced civilization, these sacrifices would be symbolised by dancers, almost in a state of trance, cutting themselves and offering their blood to the gods.

The first attempts at what we to-day call mimic dances, executed mainly with a view to diverting the audience and lending an air of festivity to certain tribal ceremonies or religious celebrations, took the form of nature-imitations.

The dancers of the Arunta tribe of Australia still perform a dance, imitating their totem-bird, the emu, in which they clownishly stretch their necks, scratch the ground with one leg, and indicate with a wealth of unnecessary gesture that an egg has been laid. There is a curious similarity between many primitive dances, which survive to-day in countries with no external cultural intercourse whatsoever.

Take, for example, a dance of the inhabitants of the Indonesian Mentawei islands, with its imitation of a hen chasing her chicks and spreading her wings over them when the hawk appears. There is a similarity of feeling between this and the aboriginal emu dance, both being clumsy and clownish imitations of what the natives observe in their vicinity. The same applies to yet another version of these bird-dances, that of the Batak of Central Sumatra, in which the participants adorn themselves with realistic bird masks and beaks for their performance of the hornbill dance.

The similarity between folk art in various unconnected countries may go even further, without the slightest trace of a connecting link being evident, either in the past or in the present. The following anecdote may illustrate the point.

When Antonia Mercé, the celebrated la Argentina, went back to her native country after many years in Europe, she was taught an almost extinct native dance by an old hag of a South American tribe, which traced its lore back to the Incas. She found that the steps and the accompanying dance-song had a similarity with the *Gopak* from Southern Russia. Equally striking was the fact that the authentic costume given to her for this dance had red and yellow embroideries with stylized motifs, commonly used in Russian peasant art.

Another striking example of these similarities is found in certain nostalgic tunes of the Basque country, a country with a very ancient language and a mysterious past, which local belief claims to be linked up with the mythical lost continent of Atlantis. The Basques accompany their ballet-like folk dances, of great variety and beauty, with singing. These songs seem almost to be copied from certain Caucasian folk-songs, both as regards the melody and the meaning of the text. The boys, with neat and nimble footwork, perform not only such intricate steps as the *pas de bourrée*, which we know to be derived from folk dancing, but also *entrechats* and quick double turns, steps rarely, if ever, encountered in this kind of 'natural' dancing.

These frequent and inexplicable similarities, baffling the ethnologists as much as the historians, have given rise to much speculation. There is an

1. Cambodian Temple Dancers, bas-relief in Angkor Vath

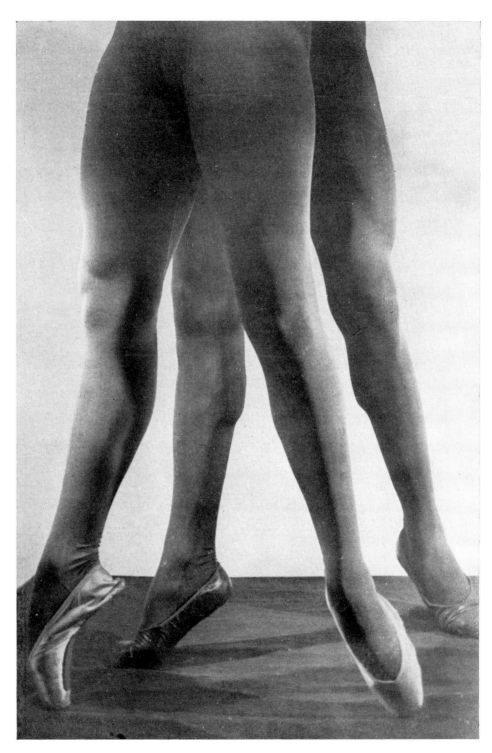

2. Pas de deux: Points and half-points

3. Pas seul: Poised on the full point

4.   Marie Taglioni in 'La Sylphide'

attractive theory that elementary human emotions form the universal basis from which racial variations develop. The simpler and more elemental the emotions—exultation, depression, superstitious awe, wooing, etc.—the more chance there is of a similar stylization of universal expression, particularly when this spontaneous expression takes the form of an unskilled dance.

EVOLUTION

Some of the oldest records of the dance which we possess are to be found in the Bible. The children of Israel, performing group dances round the Idol of the Golden Calf, and the solo dance of the prophetess Miriam, performed to the greater glory of God, and accompanied by the eerie tones of the flutes, must have contained in rudimentary form some of the material from which our more complicated present-day dances are derived. Our various forms of folk-dancing, as well as the more studied performances of the trained artists of the theatre, emanate from these sources.

The main authentic records we possess of the dances of ancient times are to be found in the decorations on Greek and Roman pottery which portray pagan dances of nymphs, fauns, and satyrs playing *pastorales* upon reed-pipes. Though some of the sacred temple dances of those times were rituals with a profound religious meaning, there were others of a less sacred character, as, for example, the suggestive dances of the hetairae, aiming at sensuous appeal only. In the classic tragedies of Aristophanes and Sophocles the chorus commenting on the stage drama must also have performed slow group movements. In the comedies of Plautus, as well as during certain sacred spring rituals, the more lascivious movements of the Bacchanalia were introduced. But in the main these earliest theatrical dances must have been purely decorative, and only incidental to the development of the action on the stage, which was conveyed mainly by word of mouth. There was as yet no question of choreography, nor of any interpretation of the music. As for the latter, we know for certain that the rhythm was marked by the use of drums and the crotalum, a kind of silver handbell.

Elements, both of the stately decorative dances and of the more abandoned ones, leading up to a frenzy or an orgy, are present during the development of the dance in subsequent centuries. Let us imagine Apollo and Dionysos holding hands as the religious fury turns to a ritual orgy of sensual ecstasy. Satyrs and fauns, bacchantes and nymphs whirl in a frenzy of dancing, a glorification of the gods of fertility, dancing until a state of trance is reached, dancing to bring on a state of hypnosis.

In Bali to-day they still dance with the holy sword, and practise self-mutilation in the kris dance. Then there is the mad whirling of the dervishes, with its mystic intensity and its concentration of will-power, spurring them on to superhuman feats of physical endurance. In the same category are the fire dances of the Tamils of India, who dance unharmed over smouldering logs. All to the greater glory of Allah, of Vishnu, or of Shiva, and to all the other dark gods of blood, fertility and lust. Men deified and danced to the elements of water and fire. Prompted by their primitive awe of the Unknown, and their mystic leanings towards a liberation of the spirit, they used the dance merely as a means of reaching those pathological borderlands which are the extreme limits of emotional expression.

Down the ages these emotions have been mastered, subdued and stowed away in our subconscious minds. Their rudimentary elements, however, remain in the more civilised and cultured dancing of to-day. They reappear, these elements of darkness, fear, neurosis and suppressed hysteria, in contemporary stage presentations, whether modern-academic ballet or the free movement of the Central-European schools. They have been triumphantly mastered and artistically subdued in those mighty ballets of our modern repertoire of Russian ballet, *Les Noces* and *Le Sacre du Printemps*. They appear super-elegant and sophisticated, but a trifle decadent, in the ballets *Les Biches*, *Le Train bleu*, and *Pas d'Acier*, truly reflecting the spirit of an era in the last period of the Diaghilev company. And they were rather too obvious sources of inspiration to the founders of the German school, Rudolph von Laban and Mary Wigman.

MUSICAL INTERPRETATION

There is, in our dancing of to-day, a close connection between the rhythmic movement and the melody, between the dance-tempo and the beat of the music. This correlation between the movement and the rhythm of the accompanying instruments certainly existed in ancient styles of dancing and still persists in certain primitive styles. Practically all folk-dances and tribal dances of a primitive type are not only accompanied by music, be it only dance songs, but are also regulated by the pulsation of drums, or other instruments, which mark the rhythm and the time.

It may be safely presumed that the dance in its primary form was without music, prompted mainly by this elemental and instinctive urge to express different emotions through movement—muscular effort counterbalancing and working off nervous brain-tension. Later the more complicated, imitative forms appeared, directly leading towards the 'interpretative dances' with a studied and fixed choreography. The latter we find in modified and perfected form on our stage to-day, both in solo and group dances. The main difference is that our conception includes an appreciation of the music, which should give the impetus for the interpretation and determine its character.

Eventually, music became an integral part of the dance creation, dominating and directing the movement; Terpsichore, from being the mistress, became the handmaiden. As soon as music took first place it regulated the various styles of dance-form. The minuet and pavane, for example, were both Court dances, and it was the musical form alone which determined the conventional dance form to be used. The rudiments of a second, and still prevailing school of thought gradually emerged, its aim being to make plastically evident the very meaning of the music, not with the help of a mimed ballet-plot alone, but through fluid movements, emanating as it were from the very heart of the melody and prolonging the sensuous vibrations of the tune into the realm of sight: plastic visualization. From the eardrum and from the retina of the eye the significance of the melodic beauty is conveyed to the brain, and the possibility of understanding and enjoying the music is doubled.

Thus we observe how the complicated theatrical dance performances of to-day have borrowed elements from the folk dance and the conventional classic dance forms, as well as from the ancient art of miming a story and the elaborate ceremonies of Court dancing. The finished product of the twentieth century has reaped benefits from theatrical experiments of the past, and from the improvement of stage techniques, particularly lighting. And the prevalent present-day creations of modern academic ballet, which may be considered as the highest form of this art achieved so far, have also benefited from the past. It presents the sum total of the slow evolution from the barefoot dancing of the primitives to the cultivation of 'point' technique and classic ballet tradition, with its insistence upon the predominance of musical interpretation.

Music, therefore, has completely come into its own as an integral part of the ballet. The few attempts made in our days to create stage dancing without music have not been satisfactory, though some movements done to the beat of percussion instruments may have been effective.

BIRTH OF BALLET

Classic ballet proper was first heard of in the fifteenth and sixteenth centuries at the Italian and Spanish Courts. Prior to the establishment of its technique of traditional movement, dance entertainments of a lavish character were given, such as the masques at the Court of Queen Isabella. Cervantes, the immortal creator of 'Don Quixote', speaks in his chronicles of the *danzas habladas*, which were performed officially at royal receptions. These 'spoken dances' must have been rather akin to our pantomimes, with the chorus executing group dances, a few solo leads carrying the choreographic plot, and other actors explaining the action in verse and song. Their subject matter was mostly allegorical, borrowed from Grecian myths and, as Cervantes states himself, often full of easy symbolism made to order, glorifying the power and wisdom of the King and the Queen, without whose patronage these costly masques could never have been performed.

The wheels of cultural history revolve. Just before the war some supermodern ballets were announced, with the daring innovation of singing added to the symphonic score. Choirs behind the scenes, or even on the stage, lent power and dramatic intensity to the group movements. This treatment bears a similarity to the *danzas* described by Cervantes.

Indeed in his time the histrionic arts were frequently considered to be of the lowest, and the wandering groups of jesters, jugglers and actors were held in as ill repute as the dancers. They performed in the open, generally during fairs. The lowly artists who passed their own frontiers to wander through Western Europe were mainly Italians and Spaniards. The former were born singers, and the Spaniards with their peculiar and little-known castanet playing were generally cast as dancers.

This rather crude entertainment in which, all the same, we may recognize the foundation of ballet art, evolved to a higher plane with the costly and spectacular Court productions of the seventeenth century in France. The *Roi Soleil*, Louis XIV, derived this name from a ballet written especially for him, in which he appeared in person as the Sun in an allegorical dance. He commissioned the magnificent palace of Versailles to be built, with its intimate theatre and its extensive terraced gardens, planned by Lenôtre, the great garden-architect, who landscaped parts of the garden with a special view to open-air performances. On these terraces many spectacular ballets were performed. Simultaneously a ballet school was founded and a new dance tradition of a highly cultured type was born. The time was ripe for the appearance of a significant figure like Noverre.

TECHNICAL FOUNDATIONS

Jean Georges Noverre (1727-1810), the French dancer and choreographer, has been called the father of the ballet. He travelled throughout Europe teaching in many different ballet schools, and his lasting influence on the French ballet—and through this on all ballet—is evident to this day. In his *Letters on Dancing and Ballets*, published in 1760, he laid down once and for all the basic principles of ballet technique. He put form and movement on a scientific foundation, advocated more dramatic intensity of individual interpretation, and held out a warning against a mere virtuoso technique, which even then threatened to weaken ballet artistically and lower its level.

He studied the possibilities of gyration, elevation, and the gliding of the human body. He experimented to determine which stretching and bending exercises would give the greatest suppleness to the limbs, in order to obtain the most perfectly controlled *arabesques* and a maximum of endurance. He laid down the law about such movements as *pirouettes, entrechats* and *fouettés*, now stand-bys of every academic dance form. In short, he laid the scientific foundation of ballet movement, and these basic principles have remained unaltered through the centuries, and still guide every dancer, no matter how free his or her interpretations may be. No disciplined stage movement which aims at 'making music visible' can do so efficiently, effectively and harmoniously, without adhering to at least some of Noverre's basic rules. Neglect of these rules leads to distortions of the body and the flaws of a faulty technique, as used in the Central-European system, not only composing a less satisfying visual image, but also making for a less effective and more exacting use of the muscles of the lower limbs.

He used the concentrated strength of the male and the more fluid grace of the female dancer to evolve a series of secondary but important rules which tended towards the development of a strong foot technique (in some instances different for both sexes), a general balance of body and carriage, and harmonious arm movements. It is all based on the five positions of the feet. To these were later added the eight positions of the body. This great classic tradition has been handed down through the last two centuries and constitutes the history proper of our contemporary dance. Taught by three generations of the Vestris family, ballet-masters at the Paris Opera, it was formulated anew by Carlo Blasis, whose pupil Giovanni Lepri taught Enrico Cecchetti, ballet-master of Diaghilev's *Ballets Russes*. Cecchetti, in his eighties, schooled some of the great ones of our post-war world, Dolin, Massine, Markova and Lifar. These artists, whether working with American, British, French or Russian companies, keep the great tradition alive, ready to hand it over to their successors in their turn.

The male dancer was principally used as *porteur* when partnering the ballerina. The latter was allowed to shine and attract all the attention, supported as she was by the muscular strength of the man in the background, who had to do all the 'donkey work' unostentatiously. He would come into his own again, however, when demonstrating in solo dances the supreme control of the body, which is essential in a more virile interpretation of the orchestral score.

These interpretations, seemingly effortless, should never degenerate into empty athletic exhibitions, the more tempting for the male dancer as they will always secure him the audience's favour, which is too often denied him otherwise because of prevailing prejudice against the profession of dancing for men. The sincere artist obeys, however, the general rule that any solo performance should remain within the dramatic sphere of the ballet ensemble, always in close connection with the music and seemingly dependent on the music.

It was only in 1826 that the technique of the *pointes*, wrongly associated with *all* classic ballet, was perfected. Marie Taglioni, the greatest dancer of her day in Paris, first perfected the technique of using the point of the foot, which is encased in the stiffened end of the flexible ballet shoe and is supported by it, thus making pirouetting and turning easier. The men, though they were supposed to master this technique in ballet-class, were seldom allowed to use it on the stage, as it was considered effeminate. The practical consequence of this elevation on the point was an artificiality of movement, a greater fluidity of line, and an etherealization of the body, tending towards idealizing the female form and transforming its primary sensuous appeal into a more abstract, unsexed appreciation of style and refinement.

Both men and women, in these highly cultured dances of intentional and carefully balanced artificiality, would become symbols rather than living actors, depicting romantic stage sentiments rather than naturalistic ones. There was a stage reality and a stage behaviour consciously different from life. The figures were propelled, as it were, into space by the force of the music, from which all their emotions were born. They were spurred on, as if without their own volition, by its rhythm, to weave their intricate patterns of light and colour, gesture and movement, before the footlights.

The imposition of the *tutu*, or wide gauze skirt, first almost worn to ankle-length, masked the curve of the hips and emphasized the two completely separated vehicles of rhythmic expression: the lower and the upper limbs. It added to the effect of 'de-feminization', making the romantic ballerina into a symbol of unearthly beauty, hardly touching the ground when spinning on her *pointes*.

The *tutu* of this type is today mainly used for the romantic *ballet blanc*, and eternally glorified by the painter Degas. It held its own throughout the nineteenth century, when Victorian modesty forbade shortening the skirts too much. When a character dance or a national dance made a change of apparel necessary, headgear and bodice were slightly altered, but the wide skirt remained. Gradually, however, its length was shortened until it became the short frilly skirt above the knees, which is mainly used today for the classic-type of ballet, as it gives the ballerina greater scope to add impeccable line-design of the limbs. It also affords greater freedom in the *pas de deux* work, with its ever-increasing demands of technical perfection on the dancers.

CODA

Though it took another hundred years, and the birth of the modern twentieth century ballet, fathered by Serge de Diaghilev, to realize a complete artistic interpretation of the very soul of music, it has been Noverre's great merit to raise ballet in the first instance from a mere gaudy Court amusement, performed for the benefit of lordly benefactors and patrons, to a higher cultural and intellectual level.

None of his original choreographies have survived, and from the few documents available little information is to be gathered. Judged by our standards, the performances of Noverre's time and the rather involved ballets of the second half of the nineteenth century may not have been soul-stirring, but they marked at least another milestone on the road towards artistic maturity. Choreography became more elaborate, costumes and *décor* ever more lavish, until barbaric opulence and the abuse of stage effects and tricks threatened to bring the entire ballet out of focus. Furthermore, the performance of the prima ballerina was over-emphasized. Stars were made overnight, not by merit of their art alone, but because other and more decisive influences were at work to favour a particular dancer. The part the ballerina played destroyed the carefully built-up balance taught by Noverre, either because of her lack of talent, or because of her insisting on performing long solo dances, interpolated into the ballet, and serving only to exhibit her own virtuosity.

Serge de Diaghilev's famous ballet company, with which he took Paris by storm in 1909, established once more certain fundamental rules, to which he added the new factor of complete collaboration between composer, *décor* artist and choreographer. This happy intermarriage of the three arts has fostered a closer artistic interpretation of the music, both in ballet and solo dance, than ever before, faithfully rendering the atmosphere, colour, style, and the very essence of the melody.

This, then, has been the valuable contribution of the first half of our twentieth century to the historical development of ballet art, and the secret of its rejuvenation. Hence a revival of interest in the potentialities of the dance all over the world.

An ever increasing stream of detailed handbooks and specialised works on the ballet floods the bookshops all over the world. The popularity of well-illustrated monthly publications on the dance runs parallel with the ever-growing popularity of ballet. Some countries such as France and England also produce expensive publications in limited editions, often mainly consisting of reproductions, in half-tone and colour.

Of the many prominent writers of today a few will be mentioned.

Cyril Beaumont's works are put at the head of the list, as his merits both as a critic, historian and author are manifold. His *Romantic Ballet* and his *History of the Ballet* cover the whole field.

Arnold Haskell is to-day perhaps the most prolific author on the ballet. He is unrivalled as a writer on the development of contemporary Russian Ballet of the Western world. His *Balletomania* and the popular Penguin edition of his book, *Ballet*, are both comprehensive. The first 1947 edition of his *Ballet Annual*, which has been contemplated for years, set a high standard of dance chronicles and has now indeed become an annual event.

New York's Anatole Chujoy compiled a stupendous reference work in his *Dance Encyclopedia* and John Martin, most knowledgeable of critics, described many memorable events of the American dance world in his ballet books.

A few dance directors, America's Lincoln Kirstein and England's Dame Ninette de Valois, gave valuable sidelights on their own work in their books; and some dancers and teachers wrote comprehensively on their art. Elsa Bruneleschi on her Spanish Dance, La Meri on the art of the Oriental dancing, Dolin and Lifar on their craft; the former on the art of partnering of which he is an expert, the latter on his choreographies and his conception of a rejuvenated classic ballet.

André Levinson was one of the best-known writers on all the various aspects of the dance in pre-war days. His major work, published in Paris, is *La Danse d'Aujourd'hui*.

Personally I prefer the philosophical Adrian Stokes who has made penetrating studies of the dance in *Russian Ballets* and *To-night the Ballet*.

Among the younger ones Caryl Brahms and Grace Robert are outstanding. The *Borzoi Book of Ballet* contains a survey of all the better known ballets of the contemporary repertoire. In this book Miss Robert has given a comprehensive outline of the plots and the history of their performance. Caryl Brahms has been noted for her excellent *Footnotes on the Ballet* and, in a more frivolous vein and in collaboration with her late husband, she has given us those irresistible ballet classics of detective fiction: *Bullet in the Ballet*, and *Six curtains for Stroganova*.

Handy and small publications are Kay Ambrose's *Ballet Lover's Pocket Book* and the subsequent *Ballet Lover's Companion*, which contain illustrations explaining the rudiments of ballet technique in a clear and simple way. And finally, no earnest student of the dance should omit to read Noverre's celebrated *Letters on Dancing*, the credo of a great dancer and choreographer of the eighteenth century.

CHAPTER TWO

CLASSIC AND ROMANTIC BALLET

Classic ballet is to the dance, what poetry is to literature
From an interview with Diaghilev

WHAT'S IN A NAME?

THE history of the romantic ballet might be said to contain the greater part of the history of the classic ballet. There is, indeed, often a confusion of terms when dealing with the two, because they are so closely related to each other.

In ballet terms classicism connotes the clearly regulated control of each movement, as laid down by the choreographer. He imposes on the dancer control of the muscles and control of expression, in accordance with the traditional technique created by former generations. He does this primarily to further his own ends of achieving a unity in the interpretation of the ballet. The choreography may be of his own devising, or not. If it is, he is both composer and conductor of the dancers at his disposal; if it is not, he is mainly the ballet master.

The task of the ballet master or mistress does not only include the drill of the dancers, and the giving of the daily classes. It also involves recreating existing ballets which he probably knows for having danced in them himself once. When his memory fails him there is generally a dancer available who is able to supply the missing turns, or he fills these gaps in himself by making new passages in keeping with the music and the general style of the work. This is often done on purpose, to suit the particular abilities of the main dancers—smaller companies often have to rely on simplification of certain passages as arranged by their ballet master, to get by.

Then, of course, there is the system of dance annotation. We all know that this has proved a tricky problem throughout the centuries. As early as 1588 Thoinot Arbeau published his 'Orchésographie' in Paris. All through the 17th and 18th century dancing masters have described their ballets, drawing floor-plans, making design of the positions of the feet, and the posturing of the body. Up till quite recently, however, choreographers and their pupils mainly relied on their memory, to re-create existing ballets. Some dance directors have an almost photographic memory. A famous example is Marie Rambert, who seems to know by heart every note and every step of the fifty-odd ballets in her present repertoire.

In the period between the two world wars the renovator of the German dance Rudolph von Laban invented and perfected his semi-scientific system of dance annotation, his 'Schrift-Tanz'. Although effective it seems long-winded and clumsy at first sight, and it takes quite some time to get familiar with the symbols. He roughly represents the body of each dancer by a square with various symbols representing gravitation, tension, relaxing, and the different positions for all parts of the body. In the more progressive American dance faculties the reading as well as the much more difficult writing is now part of the general training.

Between these various systems of annotation and the smallfilm, which can give an idea of the floor pattern of the group, as well as of the details of the solowork, the preservation of individual dances and performances seems now assured.

The classic ballet evolved from the pageantry of Court dances and had achieved a definite form of its own before the advent of the romantic era, which coincided with the invention of dancing *sur les pointes*. In the early part of the nineteenth century, when romantic feeling pervaded all art, the idea of a more exact interpretation of the moods of music germinated. Most of the ballets of those days were classic in form, and became romantic in their performance. The classic repertoire of the twentieth century has two components: the romantic ballet—either surviving in its original form, or developed from it—and the contemporary academic ballet, non-romantic in feeling but basically classic in technical execution.

This, obviously, does not mean that a romantic choreography could not be created to-day. Indeed it sometimes is. A new *ballet blanc* could be created as well in 1980 as in 1850. It is the nature of the ballet theme rather than its technical form which decides its classification. When the sense of form is stronger than the sense of musical colour it may be called classic. When the musical colour dominates and the lyrical interpretation over-shadows the sense of form, it may be called romantic. Further, when abstract or contemporary themes are used, sometimes violently naturalistic, with a classic technique incorporating some of the freer movements, the term of modern-classic, or, as some prefer, modern-academic, may be applied.

The creation of this last form leads automatically towards the present controversy between the lovers of the clear and pure classic ballet and those who prefer the more varied, emotional, and perhaps intellectually superior type of the ambitious modern-academic school. The latters' argument is that a too rigid control of the dancer's interpretative powers, exercised merely to acquire a flawless but cold technique, makes for a lessening of those same interpretative powers.

Ballet, the most cultured and cultivated of the arts, has thus become highly complex in its various manifestations. Yet these are fundamentally alike, because their origin is the same. It all developed smoothly through three centuries. Let us therefore first examine its early beginnings.

BALLET IN ITS INFANCY

Court pageants of mediæval times generally consisted of a series of tableaux, in which the theme was carried by the pantomime and dancing was added merely as a pleasing afterthought. The vocabulary of the steps used was compiled from adaptations of the existing peasant-dances. These, in a more complicated or perhaps restrained form, were conquering society and the Court. Such dances as the *gigue* and the *rigaudon*, the *chaconne* and the *bourrée*, the *passacaille* and the *gaillarde*, sound familiar to us because the great composers of the day, Bach and Lully, Palestrina and Rameau, frequently used these dance metres and rhythms in their own creations.

It is remarkable that in the transference of these rustic and artless dances from village to Court profound alterations occured. The Spanish *sarabanda*, for instance, a gay and simple dance, was altered beyond recognition, until the authorities had to take it upon themselves to forbid its performance, as it was considered an exhibition of too extravagant an abandon, and liable to corrupt public morals which, in that none too prudish age, must have been able to stand up to quite severe onslaughts.

All these dances, mainly of French and Spanish origin, went into the making of ballet. The classic choreographer first aimed at perfecting their technical execution. Then he combined a series of steps belonging to different dances, in order to get a maximum of effect and to avoid the monotony which always accompanies the unskilled performance of folk-dances. He finally arranged a sequence of such of these newly combined dances as were suitable for stage presentation, and fitted in with the plot of the ballet. Let us take, as an illustration of this adaptation of folk-dances to the stage, the steps of the *bourrée*. This dance is mainly made up of the *pas de bourrée*, which originally consisted of three transfers of weight from one foot to the other. When the choreographers had done with it there were no less than twenty-three known variations of this particular step. Theatrical evolution brought it to a virtuoso perfection of artificiality, which included the very difficult running on the points, which is rarely performed to-day. Many of these dances were mainly designed to demonstrate mastery of muscle-control combined with elegance of execution and, when well done, they gave the impression of ease and spontaneous response to the rhythmic flow of the music, which is one of the secrets of an artistically satisfying stage effect.

The first ballet-masters who were responsible for the building-up of the stage presentations and the sequences of steps, had to possess profound anatomical knowledge to safeguard them against making excessive demands upon the physique of the dancers. In ballet the ability to perform mere physical feats is not enough, unless the interpretation of a particular part warrants it. Elementary ballet movements taught included rotation, elevation, jumping, throwing and holding. Stress was laid on a pure line and on *ballon*, that quality of movement which gives lightness and elasticity. Apart from these exercises in mechanical ability the artistic interpretation of feeling and musical colour was accentuated. This necessitated an infinitely more intricate development of facial and bodily expression than was originally required by rustic forms of the dance. An entirely new art of the cultivated dance was born.

DEVELOPMENT IN EUROPE

The ballet proper, as we know it to-day, was produced as early as the fifteenth century, developing from those costly and magnificent parades which included dwarfs, jesters and jugglers, as well as mimes and (acrobatic) dancers. These masques had group movements and solo dances inspired by the folk-dances of the period. The rather simple figuration of the country dances served as a basis for the more intricate steps of the stage.

The first choreographer known by name, Bergonzio di Botto, appeared at one of the Courts of Italy, and created a stir with his banquet-ballet in 1489. Italy has remained to this day a country of ballet tradition, with a history of its own, closely interwoven with that of Italian opera. Both art forms were a logical derivation from the mediæval *commedia dell'arte*. Italian ballet, however, did not produce the lasting results nor the continuity of tradition of the French school. Although in those early days there must have been travelling dance companies, going from country fair to Court festival, we only hear again specifically of an official ballet in 1581, when Catherine de Medici ordered her Majordomo to arrange: '*Le Ballet comique de la Reine*'. The only definite thing we know about it is, that it cost the grumbling tax-payers millions for its lavish display.

The composer Jean Baptiste Lulli earned popular successes with his folk-dance compositions, of which the more sedate minuets and rigaudons were also danced in Court society. Encouraged by official approval he then com-posed his first opera-ballets and also the many dance interludes in the plays of Molière. He started in 1664 with Molière's gay '*Le Mariage Forcé*', in which Lulli himself appeared as one of the dancers.

During the reign of Louis XIV, ballet came into its own, and fortunes were spent on its perfection. Under the august patronage of this monarch the *Académie Royale de la Danse*, founded in 1661, flourished and came to maturity. Some of the greatest dancers and ballet-masters of France taught in this school. After Noverre, an important director was Vestris II (1760-1842), the second brilliant member of a family celebrated for its dancing through three generations, and himself the ideal type of a purely classic *dan-seur noble*. They established rules and moulded future generations of ballerinas. After Louis XV succeeded to the throne, and during the greater part of the eighteenth century, the grandiose manner, previously favoured, was replaced by a more complicated artificiality, which added other codes of expression and more intricate dance forms to the established steps. Dancing thus reached a higher level of technical achievement, but technique for technique's sake favoured the exhibition of virtuoso turns, to the detriment of the artistic value of the spectacle. Marie Camargo (1710-1770) was the perfect expo-nent of this advanced French school, and introduced such steps as the *jetés* and the *entrechats*, now indispensable to the classical idiom. She seemed, how-ever, to possess the other rare qualities that make a dancer a great artist. She was probably the first ballerina who was allowed to be the dominating figure of the production, as she was able to stamp the entire ballet with her own personality. Up till then the first male dancer, who was in most instances also the choreographer, had assumed this role, the ballerinas often being more apt in stirring Court intrigues than in mastering the art of the pirouette.

Her rival was Marie Sallé (1707-1756). She was a very intelligent woman and remarkable for her virtuous life which, in her position in those days, was somewhat out of the ordinary. She was a great friend of Voltaire and an admirer of Jean-Georges Noverre, greatest ballet expert of his time, whose ideals she shared. They dreamed of renovating the ballet and give the dance a more profound artistic meaning. Successors of these first two famous ballerinas were the graceful Madeleine Guimard, and the rather masculine Fräulein Heinel. All through the subsequent dance history one is to meet rival dancers, who compete furiously for the favour of the public. Ballet intrigues must have started as soon as the star system developed early in the piece, often stimulating ballerinas to give their utmost through a healthy competition.

Throughout the nineteenth century this position of *prima ballerina assoluta* was maintained by the big four of the romantic epoch: Marie Taglioni, Carlotta Grisi, Fanny Elssler and Lucille Grahn. In our own century Adeline Genée and Anna Pavlova filled this role, the latter being a perfect example of a predominating *ballerina assoluta*. Somehow one hesitates to indicate the outstanding dancers of today as such, although Markova, Fonteyn, Hightower and Ulanova seem to have many of the required qualities. Today, however, they work mostly in established companies, alongside fellow-artists who maintain a high standard. Formerly however, even in Pavlova's time, the star system threw the entire stage presentation out of artistic balance, giving too much attention to the solo dancer. As the ensemble work was left too much in shadow, a lowering of the standard of the corps de ballet was inevitable in the long run... and the poor supporting male dancer became simply a ballerina's prop.

The educational value of the Paris school has remained of supreme importance through three centuries, because of its widespread influence on other schools. There appeared in Italy a renovator of ballet, Salvatore Vigano (1769-1821) who was entirely a product of the French system. Exploiting the national feeling of the Italians for melodrama, he was one of the first to compose dramatic ballets of a calibre which we would still call today eminently satisfying, if one can judge by the records left.

Many of these dance dramas—technically products of the French school— were first given at the Scala in Milan, where Vigano held the position of ballet master.

From its very inception the classic teaching of the Paris Academy was

based on the all-important five positions. These were a result of the discovery that, through a complete turn-out of the feet to 180 degrees, the weight
of the body would be equally divided over the two supporting columns of the
trunk, which made many ballet movements easier of execution. This was
first laid down in the teachings of the *Académie Royale* and made into a
standard system by André Beauchamps. His colleague, the dancer André
Lorin, then perfected this system with an attempt at dance notation, the so-
called steno-choreography. Lorin's successor as instructor at the Academy
was Octave Raoul Feuillet, who in his turn added to the system and published
it in 1701 under the self-explanatory title: '*Choréographie, ou l'Art d'écrire la
Danse*'. This now perfected French method was carried through the eighteenth century by the various members of the brilliant Vestris family, from
Gaetan Vestris, the 'God of the Dance' through his son Auguste and grand-
son Auguste Armand, also called Auguste II or Vestris III.

One of the latter's pupils was the Paris balletmaster Didelot, whose
disciple Marius Petipa (1822-1910) worked the last fifty years of his life in
Russia. Although better known as co-choreographer of the great Tchaikovsky ballets, he should be also remembered as the dominating influence of the
traditional French school on the brilliant Russian one.

The predominating world influence of French ballet was challenged, in
the past, by the Italians. The great dance technician Carlo Blasis gave, in
the middle of the nineteenth century, a new impetus to the school of Milan,
and his pupil, Giovanni Lepri, handed down the tradition to Enrico Cecchetti, who guided the first steps of such stars of to-day as Markova and Lifar,
and taught Marie Rambert. The latter, mainly responsible for the training of
most of Britain's outstanding dancers and choreographers of the pre-war and
this post-war era, has in this way handed on some of the great tradition to
British ballet which today, together with American ballet, have taken their
rightful place among the longer established institutions.

The Imperial Russian Academy of Dancing was founded in 1735, under
the direction of the French ballet-master, Landet, and with the patronage of
the Empress Anna.

This French influence predominated in Russia until the end of the last
century when, with the growing importance of the national Russian school
of music, the art of the ballet became more independent and acquired a more
marked national flavour by absorbing elements of the rich and varied Russian folk-lore and music. The school attached to the Imperial Marinsky

5. Ludmilla Tcherina and the late Edmond Audran in 'Swan Lake'

6. Ballet Rambert's pre-war solo dancers Sally Gilmour, Maude Lloyd, and Celia Franca

7. Irène Skorik in 'Aurora's Wedding', at the Paris Opera

8. The Ballet Rambert in 'Les Sylphides'

Theatre was at the time easily the most brilliant one in Europe. The teaching presented the sum total of the joint French-Italian technique, favoured since 1847 by the great ballet-master from Marseille, Marius Petipa. Eleven years afterwards he was appointed ballet-master in Russia, where he taught several generations of dancers. The school reached the peak of its glory at the turn of the century with such dancers as Vera Trefilova, Mathilde Kchesinska, Vaslav Nijinsky and Anna Pavlova appearing under the tuition of maestro Enrico Cecchetti.

The Italian Royal Academy of Dancing and Pantomime was founded in Milan in 1813. It is significant of the methods of the Italian school, with its emphasis on plastic emotional expression, that the word 'Pantomime' was stressed in the name. For some ten years the celebrated maestro, Vigano (born in 1769), taught in the school, but no really important work was done until the great dancer and choreographer, Carlo Blasis, took over in 1837. Thanks to him, the dazzling technique for which the Italians are famous was perfected.

A final mention must be made of the Scandinavian schools, more particularly represented by the Royal Ballet of Copenhagen which, after a lapse of more than a century, still shows the influence of its greatest choreographer, Auguste Bournonville, and of his Swedish disciple, Johannsen. For the last few decades Harald Lander has been its competent ballet-master and chief choreographer. Out of this school came the modern-academic group of Jean Borlin's Swedish Ballet Company, established in Paris, where it created a stir between 1920 and 1930, because of its daring experiments in what was then called futuristic *décor*, music and dancing.

AIMS OF CLASSICAL INTERPRETATION

The fundamental aim of any stage presentation attempting artistic expression should be to portray a state of make-believe, which may be naturalistic, abstract, romantic or purely farcical, so long as it is made acceptable to the spectator. Therefore, one should never accuse the ballet of being artificial, or artificially pretty. One should merely say that its artificiality was not always convincing.

How could this sophisticated form of an artistic and highly cultivated expression be anything other than highly artificial, even though it originated in the most primitive and elementary emotions? It was controlled and developed along the lines of stage convention which necessitated a different approach to life, if only because the optical illusion of the stage differs to a great extent from reality. The dance technique furnished the means of visualizing emotions in ballet terms. And these ballet terms cannot be naturalistic because all the movements are guided by laws, different from those regulating spontaneous movements. We all know that a purely spontaneous reaction on the part of an actor or a dancer on the stage seems gawky and clumsy. The ablest actors create the illusion of being spontaneous and natural because they adhere strictly to an acquired stage technique, gesture by gesture or word by word. Improvisation is always dangerous.

The make-believe of the stage is primarily brought about by the playwright and the producer, who correspond in ballet to the choreographer and the ballet-master, though the former is often his own producer and dispenses with the latter. He takes the music as his main source of inspiration to construct his ballet and build up the geometrical pattern, even if the music is commissioned for a dance theme, which has already been worked out in detail. But—and in this respect he stands alone in the world of creators— his inspiration is limited not only by the special requirements of ballet performers and technique, but also by the mechanical ability of the human dance material at his disposal. He may be compelled to mould the leading roles to his dancers, according to their abilities and limitations, instead of being able to mould his dancers to their roles. A very few of the great ones are so versatile and artistically pliable as to be able to take a wide range of parts. A *terre-à-terre* dancer who is convincing in character parts will probably lack the round purity of line and the elevation needed for the *danseur noble* of the classic repertoire.

This applies perhaps even more to mass movements, as the choreographer's inventive genius for groupings has to take into account the size and the quality of the *corps de ballet* at his disposal, which suffers in many companies from a sad inadequacy of male dancers. Unlike a play or an opera, where performers can be selected to suit the required parts, and where physical drawbacks can be overcome by outstanding talent, the ballet is, up to a point, at the mercy of its performers. Their art is less pliable than that of actor or singer. In *La Bohème* Mimi may be as bulky in appearance as her voice is in volume; but who could ever imagine a buxom Giselle going mad convincingly? Temperament and physical appearance are supremely important to the dancer, because his medium of interpretation is entirely visual. Because of this he cannot help individualizing his role. Consequently, whether he wants to or not, he dominates and modifies the choreographic quality of the ballet with his personality.

A supreme dancer like Anna Pavlova, who will forever live in the memory of those who saw her, could dominate and electrify the presentation of a third-rate ballet to such an extent that the final impression the work left was one of artistic satisfaction. On the other hand no third-rate company could aim at even superficially pleasing interpretations of famous ballets—as their technical means would make it impossible for them to adhere to the choreography, and their artistic means of expression would be hopelessly inadequate. Simplified versions of the great ballets are often performed and they may retain part of their appeal, particularly in the case of the static beauty of the *ballet blanc*. They may please the uninitiated, but to the more experienced eye the shortcomings jar, evoking a sigh for the perfection of a polished and inspired performance which can produce an intoxicating exultation which brings the true balletomane this 'drug for the soul', as Maurice Barrès has called it.

CHAPTER THREE

VARIATIONS ON A BALLET-THEME

A nation's character is typified by its dances
Confucius

NATIONAL FORMS OF BALLET

THE security and the logic of classical ballet lie in its international idiom and the universal appeal of beauty. This idiom is founded on a form of faultless mechanism which withstands all the influences of nationalism. From a purely technical point of view, subtle differences may show up in the finished products of the various schools. They are too minute, however, to be noticeable to the average audience.

Modern interpretations of classic ballet are inclined to stress national characteristics of temperament, decorative art and music. A less rigid control of dance form and expression gives scope for a more individual temperament. National composers are naturally encouraged to work for the ballet groups of their respective countries. Contemporary dance compositions are consequently very often more typical of the country of their origin than the ballets of the older repertoires.

The French school laid stress on elevation and elasticity, out of which, as a natural result, the dancing *sur les pointes* evolved. The dancers, by virtue of a severe training, became exemplary exponents of the purely classic form. The inheritance of Latin clarity and mental brilliance was shown in the inexorable logic of the dance sequences of the early classic ballet, but betrayed, perhaps, a certain coldness of feeling in the flawlessness of its geometrical design. This was often compensated by natural grace of movement and by seemingly spontaneous and effortless execution. Noverre, the great technician of this school, made each dancer, however brilliant and technically sure, adhere to his basic principles of movement. His opponents objected that he smothered individual talents with too rigid a discipline, making all efforts subservient to choreography and production. He retorted that genuine talent knows how to liberate itself from the bonds of routine. Once this high level was reached the romantic ballet appeared, laying greater stress on musical colour and the lyrical qualities of the dancer, breaking away from the cold formality of the past.

The Italian school sought its strength in brilliance and great neatness of execution, but neglected the tidy and nimble footwork which made the French method so superior. Great importance was given to the line of the gestures, and the Italian *port de bras* gave more effective arm movements than any other school. Their ballet-masters insisted on that perfect and smooth roundness of movement which other schools sometimes lack. And they certainly emphasized the importance of mimetic gestures in accordance with the exuberance of their national temperament. Mime became a separate and complete technique of stylized gestures. These inherent qualities have persisted in the dancing of the Italians, even though their ballet went into a long period of decline in 1880, from which it has not yet recovered.

The Russian school is the youngest of the three great schools of classic ballet. From its very beginning France had a strong influence on its development. The first imperial Dance Academy of St. Petersburg was founded in 1731 by the ballet-master, Landet, from Paris. The Italian influence was also soon felt and remained evident throughout, as many travelling ballet-masters taught their own systems in Russia. The Russians had few great ballet composers of their own until, at the turn of this century, Tchaikovsky, Glazounov, Moussorgski, and later Stravinsky came to the fore. At this period also costumes, *décor* and stage presentation showed revolutionary tendencies, such as those of A. Benois, Léon Bakst and Larionov. Choreography was rejuvenated by Fokine, and Serge de Diaghilev became the organizer and artistic dictator of all these talents, collaborating to bring his famous Ballets Russes into being. Supremely Russian in flavour, the dance technique at that time showed, nevertheless, the marked Italian influence of their ballet-master, Enrico Cecchetti. Technically the Russians were remarkable, as they still are nowadays. The men were notable for their elegance as *porteur* when partnering the ballerina, and for the great vigour and elevation of their jumps. The teacher of the young Nijinsky is said to have complained of 'that damned boy who refuses to come down with the others, once he is up in the air'. The women showed an amazing mastery of the technique of *pointes*. They rose smoothly onto the point of the foot, whereas the Italians were inclined to rise suddenly with a slight spring, which gave a disturbing staccato effect, but which inflicted less strain on the foot. The French, with their knack for compromise, arrived at a sensible solution by using both methods alternately, preferring a slightly less jerky spring, based, nevertheless, on the Italian method.

TRANSITION

When a tradition becomes stale it may be expected that a younger generation will baulk at its seemingly empty and outmoded forms, and will try to make a fresh start. This happened in Europe after the first World War, when the free-movement dance of Central Europe came into being. Prior to that, Jacques Dalcroze had established his music school in Hellerau, near the Lake of Geneva. Here, deviating from tradition, he attempted to free musical interpretation, and advocated natural rhythmical body movements as well. This method of eurhythmics was stripped of all convention, and had no literary associations of thought. In fact, Jacques Dalcroze was in the beginning violently opposed to this method being used by disciples in actual dance recitals. His own demonstrations were given in the open air. His *mise en scène* was the sky, rhythm, musical metre and mood—no footlights or *décor*, and no artifice or stylized expression. His methods of movement, with their different use of the muscles, and loosening up of the limbs, would confuse a classic dancer, but the physical culture technique benefited from his principles, which tended towards natural grace of bearing and of walking.

At that time a similar attempt at liberation of dance movement was made by Isadora Duncan, the Californian, whose aim was principally to arrive at a stage presentation of her own dance creations. She went back to what she considered the only original source of stylized dancing—the ancient Greek civilization. In this instance the originality, grace, and talent of an individual performer transformed public opinion for the time being, and affected the conventional outlook on dancing. This was greatly helped by the publicity which her first *succès de scandale* brought her. In those days the average audience was prudish in the extreme, and inevitably her 'bare-feet and short-tunic' dancing came in for violent criticism. Unperturbed, Duncan went her stormy way, bringing with her a vision of fresh beauty, which aired the stuffy and over-decorated drawing-rooms of her period. Her autobiography is worth reading. Though naturally biased, it gives us the detailed portrait of a woman who dared to live her unconventional life to the full, and who greatly influenced the artists of her time.

The modern schools of Central Europe deliberately broke away from all classic principles, in order to find a new medium of plastic expression, more in harmony with the agitated post-war epoch of 1918. This type of dancing has been called 'modern ballet', thus adding to the prevailing confusion of dance terms. If we want to keep to the term ballet when referring to all stage presentations with a foundation of classic technique, we should not use it in connection with the companies which use free movement exclusively. These groups preached muscle relaxation instead of the severe muscle control of the ballet. To their less disciplined dances they added physical culture movements, and also used what they could of Dalcroze's eurhythmics, in their frantic attempt to renovate the modes of dance expression completely.

The old ballet companies have since clearly demonstrated in their new works that this greater freedom of expression could also be achieved, and more effectively so, while adhering to the classic technique as a logical basis of harmonious movement. A daring experiment in abstract rendering of symphonic music such as Massine's *Choreartium*, or a modern mystical, dramatic theme such as Helpmann's *Miracle in the Gorbals*, are as stirring as any dance story that the modern expressionist groups have ever given us, with the sole exception, perhaps, of the violent satire, *The Green Table*, created by the company of Kurt Jooss.

MODERN EXPRESSIONIST GROUPS

The German Expressionist School came to life immediately after the first World War, though some attempts at finding a new dance form had been made beforehand by Rudolph von Laban, to whom we are indebted for some interesting research and experiments. The new movement was dominated by the imposing and forceful personality of Mary Wigman, who established her headquarters in Munich. Later she went to America, where she had many enthusiastic followers. Her pupil Hanya Holm founded a school in New York.

The method seemed attractive. Instead of the grind of the ballet schools, where pupils are admitted at a very early age and rarely allowed to perform professionally until, after many years, a high level of technique is reached, a free-and-easy teaching began. After a short period of elementary training the pupils were left to their own devices and inspiration. Consequently the little bare-foot dancers flourished like the green bay tree all over Europe, aiming at a maximum of effect with a minimum of technique. The bizarre and the exotic alternated with the puerile. There were also rather rare individual creations of artistic and musical integrity. Fake orientalism and the use of percussion instruments (the so-called soap-box orchestra) became the vogue. Dancing without music followed, to the accompaniment only of shuffling feet and creaking boards.

The main trouble about these new methods was that their sources of inspiration and musical interpretation were confused. Music often took second place. The dances were obscured by the incorrigible leaning of the Teutonic races towards heavy philosophy and a none too clear symbolism. The gay dances became merely coy and pretentious, lacking real sense of humour. The grave dances were too tense, developed emotionally by arduous cerebral effort. For a time they were able to hold public interest, because each new spectacle is bound to have some appeal; and snobbery played its part too. Their building went crazily up in the air, and was without the support of any foundation, because tradition was pointedly ignored. No wonder that it could not withstand the onslaught of time.

The expressionist schools favoured abrupt movements and angular lines, copied from Egyptian and Greek art. Their turned-in movements were startling and often effective. They also had a strong leaning towards the Oriental. To this conglomeration were added elements of many folk-dances. The great French-Russian critic, André Levinson, once called it the 'jerky' school. Real Nihilists of the dance, they scorned classic tradition. Their own emotions predominated, rather than those of the composer they were supposed to be interpreting. This was all very well, if their personalities were mature and sufficiently arresting, but this was rarely so.

A few solo dancers of merit emerged. Harald Kreutzberg, Yvonne Georgi, Clotilde and Alexander Sakharoff and others. They have succeeded in gaining and retaining a public of their own. Some, who won an easy success with their free-movement dances, went back later to classic ballet to improve their style. The conversion of such artists as Darja Collin and Yvonne Georgi has influenced their respective careers as choreographers to the good.

The expressionist dance school possesses at least one great choreographer. This is Kurt Jooss, who has achieved most interesting dance compositions. In its mimic force his group came near to the Italian school of mimes. At the present time, however, by repeating himself, and by making half-hearted excursions into the realm of classicism, he seems to have reached a dead end.

9. Alicia Markova and Anton Dolin in 'Sleeping Princess'

10. Ninette de Valois' ballet 'Checkmate' at the Sadler's Wells

11. Poulenc's 'Legend of the Unicorn', Paris production

13. 'Terra Australis', with the Borovansky company

14. John Gilpin, when with Ballet Rambert, in 'Czernyana'

15. Ballet Rambert in 'L'après-midi d'un Faune', with Frank Staff and Sara Luzita

16. National Ballet of Lisbon in 'Verde Gayos'

Before the second World War he found refuge in Dartington Hall in England, from where he made his world tours with his company, whereas his partner Sigurd Leeder kept the school going. The latter is now established in London with one of the few 'expressionist schools' which are still a going concern in that country, whereas Jooss has gone back to Essen, the German town where he started his company. Some of his famous oldtimers, Noelle de Mosa, Ulla Soederbaum and Georg Alexander are with him again.

Another important group of Western Germany is to be found at the Düsseldorf opera, where Yvonne Georgi is leading the ballet section. This former partner of Harald Kreutzberg is also heading towards a fusion of the classic technique and the modern dance idiom; and the achievements of her young group have so far been most satisfying, basing their 'modern' experiments on a sound foundation of technique.

The world at large, however, is looking for a further lead in the modern field towards America. In the twenties Ruth St. Denis and Ted Shawn explored the possibilities of Oriental and ethnological dance arts, bringing some experiments to the theatre which were daring for their time. In the thirties it was mainly Martha Graham who became known as a renovator of great possibilities. Hanya Holm remained in the public eye still too much a successor of Mary Wigman, although in reality she was already perfecting a style of her own. In postwar days the fantastic successes of Katherine Dunham as a dancer, choreographer and all-round theatrical genius were only loosely linked to the American dance proper, and the same applies to the more severe black art of Pearl Primus and her dancers.

But Doris Humphrey and José Limon are slowly getting the world recognition they merit... and their experiments in adding the spoken word or the dance-song to the choreographic interpretation have been keenly watched by dance enthusiasts.

Many young ones are struggling for a recognition many of them deserve... but only the future will decide which ones will be mentioned in dance history on the same level as the great ones who have contributed to the world renovation of the dance... such as Martha Graham whose work may be as violently condemned by the ones as praised by the others... but who in any case is today outstanding as representing a modern dance idiom, which is entirely of her own making. Other youg ,,veterans'' are Charles Weidman, May O'Donnell, Iva Kitchell, Sophie Maslow, and Pearl Lang.

FUTURE

The modern academic ballet, as it is developing to-day, retains the technical basis and the rigorous control of expression and movement proper to the classic ballet. On this foundation of clarity and logic, and with the aid of the perfected technical abilities of properly schooled dancers, an entirely convincing interpretation of the music is often achieved. The high quality of the trained dance material at the disposal of the choreographer, and the whole-hearted co-operation of the best painters of our time, enable the balletmaster to achieve his objectives.

Contemporary music, which is more abrupt, more direct, more complicated perhaps, and not always as pleasing to the ear as classic music, is reflected in the stage presentation. The softer mood of Chopin's Concerto, for example, inspired choreographer Bronislava Nijinska to a ballet which was modern in its abstract construction but quite romantic in feeling, whereas the virility of Stravinsky's *Le Sacre du Printemps* calls for vigour and impetuous movement, with which to interpret the overwhelming strain of this music, entirely modern in its feeling of suspense and torment.

Contemporary ballet is directly inspired by contemporary as well as by classical music, and has thus a wider scope of interpretation. Choreographer, painter and composer work together more intimately than was usual in the past, as may be seen in the closely knit unity of many a modern production.

It is probably to the rejuvenated ballet proper, with a certain leaning towards the less conventional productions of the modern expressionist dance groups, that we will have to turn for the future development of our ballet style. Compromise, as is often the case, may here also prove to be the most satisfactory solution. It will rid the expressionist dance groups of their ruthless angularity combined with a 'highbrow' general interpretation, and of their neglect of purity of line. And it will add to the self-sufficiency and the rigid self-control of the classics a spontaneity of movement, and a more intimate contact with the colour and mood of the music, which may yet help to bring ballet closer to the heart of the masses than it is to-day.

CHAPTER FOUR

THE DIAGHILEV ERA

Diaghilev was the greatest impresario ballet ever had
Serge Lifar

THE COMPANY AND ITS LEADER

THE fantastic and legendary figure of Serge de Diaghilev towers above the mighty band of talent and genius which he gathered around him during the twenty years of his reign. Although a sybarite, art-lover and connoisseur, he was never quite the impresario, the Mæcenas, or the art critic. He had inherited the Royal tradition of the Russian princes and czars, who would create a ballet company merely in order to make them perform for their own enjoyment, and without any hint of commercialization. His retort, when he was told that the public was not up to the extremes of his productions, is celebrated: 'They will dance what I like, not what the public wants'. This explains, perhaps, how he won his battle and educated the public of 1909, illiterate in regard to ballet, into becoming the famous and smart Ballets Russes public of his last season in 1929. It included snobs, faddists and freaks certainly, but also some of the greatest artistic minds of the epoch, who were well aware of the ballet's stimulating influence.

Almost all the outstanding artists of Diaghilev's time, who on one occasion or another worked with and for him, acknowledged his faultless judgment and praised his inspiring though dictatorial personality, in spite of the fact that subsequent inevitable quarrels with him always seemed to land them eventually in the camp of his opponents. In his younger days in Russia, where he was born in 1872, he dabbled in the composition of music, and in painting. One of his earliest efforts was the organization of an exhibition of advanced paintings, which soon established him as the leader of Russia's younger artistic set. Although he himself never really created, apart from a few publications on art criticism, his genius for organization, his unfailing energy and, above all, his power of artistic discrimination and foresight, inevitably brought him the fame with which his name will ever be associated. He combined the flare of the *entrepreneur* with the instinct of the born gambler, and he handled capital with a supreme disdain for money, although he himself never had any personal fortune. He was most fortunate in being able to draw on a galaxy of native talent. The best pupils of the Imperial dance school were his for the asking.

The old Marinsky Theatre in St. Petersburg was still, at the turn of our century, demonstrating the glory of the French-Italian ballet tradition of the Russians. Ballet-master Nicholas Legat represented the Russian element and maestro Enrico Cecchetti taught the precise methods and the elaborate miming of his school. At that time there were some unusually brilliant talents in the Marinsky ballet, most of them in their early teens. Nijinsky and his sister, Bronislava Nijinska, showed all the promise they were to fulfil so gloriously in later years. Pavlova and Karsavina, so different and yet so equal in potential greatness, even then competed for places in the front rank. Olga Preobrajenska, Mathilde Kchesinska, Lubov Egorova, and Vera Trefilova, among the best Russian ballet teachers, were then in their early prime. And Michel Fokine, as early as 1907, attempted to free himself from the all too rigid academic rules, and advocated a more dramatic intensity of movement, and a greater freedom in the handling of the *corps de ballet*.

The attempt becomes familiar through repetition, since another great choreographer, Noverre, had pleaded the same cause when the Court ballet was becoming too pompous and formalized, and the cold glitter of brilliance was replacing the warm glow of the sacred inner fire. Whether Fokine was decisively influenced in his new conception of freed ballet movements by the inspired dancing of Isadora Duncan, whom he saw in Russia, is immaterial, although he himself denied it, while Diaghilev affirmed it. What concerns us more is the fact that his was the master mind behind the first choreographies of the Ballets Russes, as Paris saw them for the first time in 1909.

THE THREE PERIODS OF THE BALLETS RUSSES

When dividing the twenty years of the Diaghilev reign into three periods, we should be justified in calling the first one of these periods the Fokine epoch. This was as truly Russian as the company was ever to know. Diaghilev, the super-showman, aided by the leader of fashion and society, Robert de Montesquiou, brought Russian opera to Paris during the 1909 season, together with a full ballet company, which formed an integral part of the presentation of such operas as *Prince Igor*, in which Fokine's *Polovtsian*

Dances became famous overnight. The dance group performed other ballets in its own right. The barbaric richness of the *décor* and costumes by Bakst in *Scheherazade*, and of Alexandre Benois in *Petrouchka*, made as great a stir as Pavlova's incredibly lovely *Swan Lake*, and the sensational dancing of Nijinsky.

At that time the public was hostile to shattering innovations such as Diaghilev introduced, but he nevertheless went whole-heartedly into the battle. He expertly exploited whatever there was of snobbery and intrigue surrounding the ballet, and he probably welcomed the publicity which resulted from the scandal of Nijinsky's dancing in *L'après-midi d'un Faune*. He kept his dancers mysteriously aloof and away from the public. He himself deigned to be intimate only with the very rich and the very great of the earth, who repeatedly gave him millions to lose on some magnificent artistic venture or other. He was an exalted and lonely figure. Very few of his company really knew him. He was awe-inspiring rather than loved. He always sweated the very best out of them all—to the greater glory of the Diaghilev Ballets.

At the end of that Paris season of 1909, when the final curtain descended amidst thunderous applause, the popping of corks, and a shower of laurel wreaths, it was evident that the young company would be given no rest from its triumphs. Its influence on all the arts was to become far-reaching. For the first time in history, probably, there had been a deliberate aiming at a complete merging of all the arts into one artistic entity. The choreographer, the painter, the designer of the costumes, the writer of the ballet theme, and sometimes the composer, had all worked together. The impetus given by the music flowed, as it were, from the orchestra pit across the footlights and took possession of the bodies of the dancers, who prolonged the musical emanations and made visual the rhythm. And the feeling of the music was accentuated by curtain and backdrops, by harmonies of colour and lighting.

The art of lighting was, indeed, one of Diaghilev's particular contributions to the production, and for hours on end he would test the effect of a different colour slide or an extra reflector. His answer to a well-meaning nabob's question: 'And what are you doing in the company?' 'I am the assistant electrician', is not devoid of a deeper sense. The importance he placed upon the art of dressing the show—the scenery and the wardrobe—possibly emanated from his training as a painter. The far-reaching influence which the 'Ballets Russes style' was to have on all the arts throughout the two following decades was manifest from the very beginning.

It was during the Fokine period, which lasted until the outbreak of the war in 1914, that the modern academic ballet was evolved by him, and found its own style. He freed the *corps de ballet* from its traditional slavery, and, in that pure gem of the *ballet blanc, Les Sylphides*, he gave it an importance all its own. He showed himself to be a stylist in his best Russian vein in *Petrouchka, Coq d'Or, Fire Bird*, etc., while in *Scheherazade* and *Cléopâtre* he was Oriental. In *Carnaval* and *Spectre de la Rose* he was purely romantic, and in the last-named ballet he made use of classical technique in an unorthodox way. Created for Nijinsky and Karsavina, it had a sensational success, though in later revivals it unfortunately sometimes degenerated into a stunt ballet.

In his Oriental compositions he also made full use of the individual talents of his dancers. The barbaric richness of the Bakst *décor* for *Scheherazade*, for example, was a perfect background for the strangely decorative beauty and the regal but cold personality of Ida Rubinstein. In those first seasons her mysteriously exotic mien and superb miming earned her a success which was even greater than that of Nijinsky and Pavlova. She remained unsurpassed in roles of this type, which did not require any dancing proper.

The years before and during the first World War witnessed the triumph, the decline and the subsequent tragedy of Nijinsky. As soon as the creative urge became apparent in this dancer of unusual talent, with his inspired but entirely intuitive approach to choreography, it was clear that Fokine's star was setting, and he left the company.

Two of Nijinsky's choreographies survive, though in an entirely modified form. The most ambitious one is *Le Sacre du Printemps*, composed to Stravinsky's most intense and very Russian score. It was presented after laborious and endless rehearsals, which clearly demonstrated the typical Ballets Russes approach of intimate collaboration between the principal creators. The other one is *The Afternoon of a Faun*, done to Debussy's *Prélude à L'Après-midi d'un Faune*. It has been said that the painter Léon Bakst was responsible for many details of the choreography. It was as revolutionizing in conception as the other one, and it certainly was received with a great hostility on the part of the public, this time not so much on account of the music as because of the choreography. The phallic movements in the finale earned for it an ambiguous reputation, the flavour of which has remained even to this day in the revised versions as danced by the outstanding male dancers of to-day, Dolin, Lifar, Lichine, Eglevsky and Youskevitch.

During the difficult period of 1914–1918 Diaghilev managed to keep a depleted company together, which stayed for long periods on end in the neutral countries, Switzerland and Spain. From that time until 1920 or thereabouts extends the Massine period. It was during this phase of its existence that the name of the company could easily have been changed from 'Russian' to 'International'. Of the former Russian collaborators only the painters, Larionov and Gontcharova, his wife, remained faithful. Other painters of the time, including Picasso, Derain and Matisse, and outstanding composers such as Respighi, Fauré and Eric Satie, collaborated with choreographer Massine.

Though the soloists were mainly Russian, many minor parts were entrusted to young foreigners, who later became stars in their own right. They kept their Russian stage names, like Anton Dolin, (Patrick Healy-Kay), who ultimately succeeded Leonid Massine as first dancer. Lydia Sokolova (Hilda Munnings) and Ninette de Valois (Edris Stennus), who were to build up a new British Ballet, formed part of the company.

Massine gave in this, his early period, some of the ballets which he himself still considers amongst his best efforts. They are *The Good-humoured Ladies*, *La Boutique fantasque*, and *The Three-cornered Hat*. In the last-named he introduced authentic Spanish dance forms (the *farruca* and *fandango* are always high-lights of the performance), but he adapted them to the ballet. The company's stay in Spain, together with the endless performances of gipsy and folk-dancing which they had witnessed, helped Massine with the creation of a work which was outstandingly different. The choreography deftly translated the rich and mature score of de Falla. The name of the gipsy dancer, Felix, who taught Massine in Seville, should remain associated with the creation of this ballet.

The last period of the Diaghilev Ballet, from 1922 to 1929, was the period of intellectual approach and cerebral effort, of the *chichi*, and of the decline. It was the period of the ultra-modern in theme, music, *décor* and choreography. These elements were becoming largely intellectual in their appeal. They were mannered, experimental, and in some cases magnificently sterile. Nijinska, with her unusual talent, achieved several curious productions which truly reflected this slightly decadent period. Young composers of the brilliant French group of *Les Six*, such as Poulenc, Auric and Milhaud, came to the fore, also the very young Henri Sauguet and Vittorio Rieti.

Marie Laurencin painted the adorable pastel *décor* for Poulenc's *Les Biches*.

Jean Cocteau conceived the argument for *Le Train bleu*, which centred round the acrobatic talent of Dolin. Coco Chanel, the dressmaker, designed dance costumes. George Balanchine showed the budding of a high talent for choreography with his *The Cat* and *Le Chant du Rossignol*.

The Soviet composer, Prokofiev was commissioned to compose the score for the abstract *Pas d'Acier*, since even then Diaghilev was casting an eye towards the new Russia, with a view to showing his successes 'at home', a project which was never realized.

This longing for his native country was, perhaps, the premonition of a man who knew that he had not long to live. A man full of superstitious fear of the sea, he was taken ill in a gondola in Venice, where he was wont to spend the season on the Lido. He was a unique type of artistic dictator who combined initiative with discrimination. He commanded and lost millions with superb unconcern. He brought about the renaissance of the ballet of our own era. The work he had striven to achieve did not die with him. He had patiently paved the way for its survival. He has not lived in vain.

THE ARTISTS

The various periods of the Diaghilev company might well be marked by the starring of the successive first dancers. Nijinsky and Pavlova were the glowing lights of the pre-war period, and even when Pavlova, after her first triumphal success in Paris, decided to break away and form her own company, he still remained the greater attraction, though these last years of his reign were rather tormented, and choreographically not too happy.

Then came Leonid Massine, outstanding from the beginning both as a dancer and choreographer. Dolin succeeded him, and in the final stage the adolescent Serge Lifar made his debut. He had just started on his first choreographies at the time of Diaghilev's death. Subsequently he sky-rocketed to fame as ballet-master of the Paris opera.

From time to time controversies have been started as to the importance and the necessity of casting the male dancer as the principal figure of the ballet. Diaghilev certainly put great emphasis on the presentation of his male stars. It is, however, incorrect to assume that this was entirely due to incidental circumstances of his personal attachments. On the contrary, it was historically and logically to be expected that the major accent should be shifted back to the man, after the predominance of the ballerina, which had

17.   A Portrait study of Anna Pavlova

DIAGHILEFF, BY SEROV, 1903

18. Serge de Diaghilev, after a drawing by Serov

19. His disciples Markova and Dolin in 'Giselle'

been stressed to such an extent that the spectacle as a whole was thrown out of focus. Inevitably the male dancer was to retrieve his position sooner or later.

Outstanding personalities like Vaslav Nijinsky, who could not help but dazzle the audience with their extraordinary prowess, naturally predominated and enjoyed greater prestige than the ballerina, while in later years the more intellectual or dramatic approach to ballet actually shifted the main burden of interpretation onto the male dancer's shoulders. After all, when a *Hamlet* ballet is conceived, for example, it is Shakespeare rather than the choreographer whom we must blame for Hamlet's part being more important than that of Ophelia!

The right of the male dancer in classic ballet to aspire to first place has been questioned by a public which is ignorant of the ballet's background, history and evolution. There has been a confusion of ideas as to what is effeminate and what is graceful. Haskell, in several of his books, deals with this problem of public prejudice, and makes it quite clear.

It is not man against effeminate man, but the primitive mind against the sophisticated one. Why should grace, as an attribute of both sexes, be monopolized by the woman? The orchestration of male and female movement and personality brings out the characteristics of man and woman. When the man apes the woman the whole contrast is lost and has no longer any place in ballet. His *raison d'être* is to stand as a strong mental and physical contrast to her. He should be the lover in every movement... a conception of masculinity that may be difficult to understand in countries where, by a strange paradox, it is considered so essentially masculine for men to be happiest in the company of their own sex.

This is a comprehensive statement, and should clarify the male dancer's position. He must please. His movements must be music and grace. But one should not be deceived by mere appearances. Those silk-clad legs and languidly moving arms are springs of steel. The painted jaw juts out firmly. He lifts the woman high, and laughs as he does it. He negligently performs mighty feats of elevation. He exhibits no apparent strain in his achievement of fine athletic efforts, as do his brethren of the sporting field and the stadium.

It was typical of Diaghilev that he always knew how to gather the best artists of his generation around him, though once he had used them he often quarrelled with them irrevocably, and made them his enemies for life. But with all that he remained the motive force of the enterprise.

He was superbly served by his dancers. When Pavlova left, Karsavina took over. Then came a Nemchinova, a Doubrovska, a Spessivtzeva, and a

Danilova. He had such splendid character dancers as Woizikovsky, Idzi-kovsky and Adolf Bolm. And he was always searching for young talent. At the end of his life he cherished Lifar and Nikitana as the jewels they certainly were, and Alicia Markova, a shy English schoolgirl, who was then doing her deep *pliés* at the bar under the watchful tuition of father Cecchetti.

During this last period of tempestuous trial and seething activity the most important artists of the Paris School contributed *décor* and costumes to the ballet. This side of the ballet became indeed all-important. Utrillo, Chirico, Rouault, Braque, Miro and Juan Gris pointed the way. In the background was always the huge form of Larionov, and the watchful friendly eyes of Gontcharova, creator of that quintessence of Russian folk-art, the *décor* of *Coq d'Or*.

Throughout these years one rather unobtrusive figure remained back-stage and in the background, by profession and by choice. The public never guessed how much the success of the performance was due to the work of Serge Grigoriev, director, stage-manager, ballet encyclopædia and receptacle of many artistic—and other—secrets which are now buried in the past.

When in 1951–'52 the 'Original Ballets Russes' was revived, with a rather disappointing cast and a mainly British corps de ballet, Grigoriev and balletmistress Lubov Tchernicheva were the only members who had survived from the Diaghilev period.

Although imbued with the Diaghilev spirit of perfection they had to struggle against too many odds. However, revivals of masterpieces of former times of splendour, such as the *Coq d'Or* in the original Gontcharova presentation as commissioned by Diaghilev, showed that truly great works still hold their appeal, whatever the shortcomings of execution. The same applied to Massine's great symphonic ballet 'Les Présages' and Fokine's 'Paganini', still as moving as ever. They seemed to have a life of their own, a blaze of inspiration so vital that it would shine through at every turn, even when that turn was badly done.

SUCCESSORS OF THE BALLETS RUSSES

After the death of Diaghilev the company was disbanded and the members dispersed, some of them forming small companies of their own (Nemchinova, Spessivtzeva, etc.). The only member who found a permanent and immediate outlet for his creative abilities was the youngest of the company, Serge Lifar, who was appointed as first dancer at the Opera in Paris. He quickly rejuvenated this venerable ballet institution, as he was allowed free scope for his talents, which were highly individualistic.

With his works, *The Legend of Icarus*, performed to a special score of 'percussion and sounds', and the more orthodox *Prometheus* and *David Triumphant*, he reached the peak of his always uneven choreographic achievement. He shocked, astounded and delighted his audiences by his daring. He attempted the interesting but sterile experiment of a ballet without music, which would have been unheard-of in the sacred and conservative precincts of the Opera ballet in any other period. He remains in our memory as an unusual artist, perfectly schooled but erratic in his work. In his latest post-war period of development he seems to have re-established his waning reputation as an outstanding ballet-master. His grasp of the necessities of television technique for some work entrusted to him by the French and the British television, has been rightly applauded. Although he still dances leading roles at the Paris Opera time is naturally taking his toll, and the outstanding classic dancer of yore is no more. His latest choreographies have been uneven... his Snow White (*Blanche Neige* on a score of Maurice Yvain) was the most distinguished failure of the 1951 season; but his Don Quichote ballet (*Le Chevalier Errant*) had remarkable passages, still dominated by Lifar the choreographer, as well as by Lifar the dancer.

Lifar's intellectual approach and understanding of ballet problems is remarkable. His ideas have been put forth at length in several books. He was the first dancer ever admitted as a lecturer to a French University. At the Paris Sorbonne he gave lectures on Madame Terpsichore, a muse who had never before been taken so seriously.

To Colonel de Basil must be handed the palm for collecting Diaghilev's artistic inheritance and for regrouping the members of the wandering tribe. He continued where the master had left off, pushing ahead with the improvement which had been apparent during that last season of 1929. He procured many costumes and *décors* and (what is always a complicated task) obtained the copyrights and original choreographies of outstanding works of the Diaghilev repertoire. He was, furthermore, most fortunate in attaching the now more mature Massine to his company, whose creations maintained the high standard and the reputation of the original *Ballets Russes*, under the name of Colonel W. de Basil's *Ballet Russe*.

One of de Basil's first efforts was to present to the public his 'baby-ballerinas', Toumanova, Baronova, and Riabouchinska. As they are now, all in separate companies, at the peak of their fame and at the top of their profession, it is perhaps premature to attempt an assessment of their exact place in ballet history, which they helped to make. But it is clear that they will be classed among the great ones of the epoch, even as Massine will be considered one of the few who possess genius. Among other young dancers of the front rank were Lichine, later a rather uneven choreographer in his own right, Shabelevsky, Eglevsky, Youskevitch, Nina Verchinina, Vera Zorina and the exotic Sono Osato.

Differences of opinion and other difficulties led to disruption of the company, and to a regrouping, such as one frequently witnesses in the world of the dance. René Blum, brother of the one-time premier, Léon Blum, and director of the Monte Carlo Theatre, took over one half in 1936, and attached Fokine to the new company, which was called René Blum's *Ballets de Monte Carlo*. It was later absorbed by the *Ballet Russe de Monte Carlo* when another reshuffling had taken place.

Fokine presented a new arrangement of *Les Sylphides* and created important works, such as *Don Juan*, on music by Gluck, and *L' Epreuve d' Amour*, an exquisite *chinoiserie* on music by Mozart, with lavish *décor* and costumes by André Derain.

Massine, who had delighted the ballet world with his monumental symphonic *Choreartium* and *Les Présages*, now created exquisite ballets in a lighter vein, such as a new version of *Le beau Danube*, and Offenbach's *Gaieté Parisienne*. Balanchine scored with two works of merit, *Cotillon* and *Concurrence*, in which his power of vision was apparent, though there was only a slight indication of the quality of lyric classicism with which his later works are pervaded. It has been argued, concerning the works of these two outstanding choreographers, that they were both poetic, pictorial and mundane. We will try elsewhere (in Chapter IX) to define Balanchine's and Massine's approach more clearly. The influence which their work had, and still has, on the development of our coming choreographers merits a more detailed description.

Our post-war period is seeing a rather confusing number of companies in which the many brilliant young American and British dancers almost outnumber the Russians.

In Europe some companies are static and long established. The Royal

Danish Opera Ballet is quietly continuing a tradition of centuries, as is of course the Paris Opera Ballet... with an improved ballet company at the second subsidised state theatre, the Opéra Comique, doing excellent work with ballet-master Jean-Jacques Etcheverry.

In England the Sadlers Wells ballet, and the secondary but by no means second-rate company of the Sadlers Wells Theatre ballet is firmly established. International Ballet and Ballet Rambert seem to follow the itinerant career of the Champs Elysées Ballet, touring incessantly. Dolin's *Festival Ballet*, now devoid of the services of the incomparable Markova, works along the same lines.

In the States some of the companies have swept the European field, such as *New York City Ballet*, and the fine *Ballet Theatre*. The *Ballet of the Marquis de Cuevas*, which had its artistic ups and downs, might all the same be called a successor to the Diaghilev tradition, if only because its director can find continuous financial support. Rosella Hightower and Serge Golovine have established themselves in the frontrank, with Skibine emerging as a choreographer of great promise. Ballerinas with an American training, the Tallchief sisters and Alicia Alonso, have now also been accepted as world personalities of the ballet.

CHAPTER FIVE

THE TWENTIETH CENTURY

He who danceth not knoweth not the ways of life
Persian Proverb

REVOLT AGAINST ACADEMIC PRINCIPLES

ALL through the history of ballet, as its innovations and developments have shown, each succeeding generation has been prompted by a desire to break away from the tradition of its forbears. This led to the triumph of romantic ballet, its subsequent decline in the second part of the last century, and its renaissance in our own times.

The year 1661 marked the first important milestone on the road of development. The French Academy of Dancing gave an official status to the least acknowledged of arts.

The year 1760 marked another major event: the publication of Noverre's *Letters on the Dance*, calling for a halt in the quest for perfection of technical ability for its own sake, at the expense of depth of feeling.

Some people regard the year 1826 as momentous in the history of technical development. It was then that Marie Taglioni, the genius of romantic ballet, used 'full points' for the first time. Though 'half-points' and even 'three-quarter points' had been used long before that, this supreme elevation on the part of the female dancer established her pre-eminence beyond question, and for the time put the male dancer completely in the shade.

Isadora Duncan was the precursor of 'free movement' and of 'expressionist' dancing. Her first visit to Russia took place in 1907, when Fokine was doing his first choreographies. He has shown a marked evidence of Duncan's freedom of movement in his style ever since, and has pointed the way for his younger colleagues to exploit all the possibilities of this new style within the limitations of classic ballet.

It took the gigantic upheaval of the first World War, and a bolder expression of revolutionary tendencies by the new generation, to establish the 'modern dance' firmly. The Central-European movement was born in Germany, where social despair was at its deepest. Honestly destructive as they were, they denied all principles on which academic ballet had been built, and with only an obscure philosophy to guide them, they started all over again from the very beginning. Their entirely intellectual approach to the dance lacked elevation of spirit and soul.

A violent reaction resulted in the world of arts in general and in the dancing academies in particular. This eventually led to a rejuvenation within the threatened and sacred precincts of classical ballet, which needed, perhaps, this outside stimulus to stir it from its self-sufficiency.

For several decades the two schools were strongly opposed to each other. Judging the struggle over a period of time, with the perspective of the second World War closing another era, we must admit that both have influenced each other to a marked degree, whether they liked it or not.

MODERN-ACADEMIC BALLET

Traditional ballet has absorbed the best elements and principles of the free-movement schools. It has been vitally affected by all the art movements of to-day, from cubism and surrealism to the very latest rational romanticism.

It has not given up a single one of its own basic principles; it has merely, and wisely, enriched itself by a more lenient attitude towards reform, which gives the choreographer a greater scope for experiment. In this way it has become more and more a chronicler of its time, reflecting the inner turmoil and turbulence of modern youth. The aristocrat has left the royal Court to come among the people—perhaps because Courts are no longer the fashion. This gesture should remove, once and for all, the stigma laid on ballet of exclusiveness and of providing highbrow entertainment only for the chosen cultured few.

The new arts and new trends in literature towards abstract renderings of artistic inspiration have fostered the 'literary' and 'abstract' ballets such as Massine's much discussed symphonic masterpieces of the past—the dramatic ballets of Helpmann and Antony Tudor, and the political ballets of Soviet Russia of the present day.

The free-movement dance groups, with the sagacity which only experience and maturity can bring, seem to have acknowledged one by one that there is much in the self-imposed control of movement and expression, proper to classic ballet, which could be beneficial to their own less orthodox presentations.

They have also found that it is not so easy to break away from a foundation of movement technique which, ever since it was laid down in the seventeenth century, has been accepted by ballet-masters who, with all their experience, ought to know what they are about! Irrespective of whether the dance is done with bare feet or in the padded ballet shoe, the artistically most convincing dance form of to-day is still founded on this formal and classic conception—the eternal five positions which are the basis of all technique—modernized though it may be.

PRE-WAR DEVELOPMENT

During the important years of evolution between 1930 and 1940 the world renaissance of the ballet favoured the individual efforts of several countries. Up to that time their artists had been schooled abroad, in France, Italy or Russia, the three powers holding the monopoly of academic training, and offering the best opportunities for gaining stage experience with the big international companies.

The World Exhibition in Paris in 1938 saw for the first time a friendly competition between various national ballet companies of the smaller countries, who followed the classic tradition and whose artists had been trained academically. It also introduced variety by the presentation of a few of the recognized expressionist groups, among them the company of Kurt Jooss and the Swiss group of Trudy Schoop.

By this time the Polish National Ballet had come into being, with such stars as Zizi Halama and Felix Parnell, and with Bronislava Nijinska as its choreographer and general director. The company introduced the work of the then litte-known composer, Szymanowski, in a folk-ballet, and won recognition with a new Polish version of the Faust legend. One of their major contributions was Nijinska's version of Chopin's piano concerto. Each variation was danced by groups of male and female dancers, whose tunics made contrasting colour schemes of graduating shades, which were in harmony with the opposing rhythms and counter-rhythms of the score. Unfortunately the times were not favourable for new and costly enterprises in Central Europe, and the excellent elements of the new company were dispersed. Nijinska's own Paris group, which was remembered for a daring presentation of *Hamlet*—preceding Helpmann's sensational version by some ten years—had previously met with the same fate.

21.   Tamara Toumanova, ballerina assoluta in the great tradition

The Cage; a daring choreography of Jerome Robbins, with Nora Kaye in the principal role

23. Australian character dancer Jon Marten in the expressional dance 'Morbidezza'

The Sadler's Wells company, which in 1938 had definitely emerged from its infancy, might already have been called the British National Ballet. It possessed an experienced director and an inspired choreographer in Ninette de Valois, and very promising dancers, such as Margot Fonteyn, Pamela May, June Brae, and Harold Turner. Robert Helpmann and Frederic Ashton were as yet choreographers in embryo. Of the repertoire, Ninette de Valois' very British period-ballet, *The Rake's Progress*, inspired by Hogarth's paintings, was outstanding. Other interesting creations were *Job* and the charming *The Gods go a-begging*. The solo dancers mentioned showed the promise which later they realised so fully. As for the *corps de ballet* of this first decade, one felt that the ethereal grace of the Russian *corps de ballet* was no fair standard of comparison for these 'healthy, rotund English girls'.

Catherine Littlefield's Philadelphian Ballet is recalled as an example of the many American efforts in the field of the classic dance. Revealing, as it did, a high standard of dancing to these pre-war European audiences, it showed the even more important fact that there was vitality and originality galore in those American-style ballets. There was the *Barn Dance*, with the local beaux and belles of the Middle West, the chattering housewives and the Paul Jones group dances. There was the witty *New York Grand Terminal*, with the train from Reno arriving, the negro carriers, the sweepers and the skit on a press interview with a Hollywood star. There was clever characterization and mime. Her company could, however, not compete as yet with Balanchine's more mature American Ballet, which consisted partly of Russian-born and Russian-trained dancers, and which, at the climax of its career in 1937, gave a successful Stravinsky festival.

Europe possessed other ballet companies, mostly attached to the respective national operas. The Latvian Ballet of Riga performed in its own right. Prague, Copenhagen, Vienna and Berlin had opera ballet with a standard repertoire, which contributed few original works of significance.

In this survey mention must be made of yet two other companies, already defunct in 1938. The first one was Jean Borlin's Swedish Ballet; the other, the company of Ida Rubinstein. Both had ample financial means at their disposal.

Jean Borlin's company was sponsored by the Mæcenas Rolf de Maré, who later founded that admirable Paris institution, the Archives Internationales de la Danse, which contained the unique collection of Pavlova's relics, and the interesting pictorial documents the Borlin company left behind, after the premature death of its leader [1]. Borlin encouraged cubists and surrealists to work for him, experimenting to his heart's content. He himself was neither a great dancer nor a choreographer of profound significance, but some of his creations, which were violently modern for his time, showed a true pioneer spirit. Léger, Braque and Picasso contributed *décor*, Milhaud and Honegger important music. His *El Greco* ballet, his *Skating Rink* and his ballet conception of the creation of the world, *L'Homme et ses Désirs*, had the merit of daring originality.

Ida Rubinstein's productions were on an even larger scale. This tall, stately mime gained her fame in Diaghilev's opulent oriental productions. As Cléopâtre and Zobeïde she found roles which suited her temperament and highly decorative personality, and which made no undue demands for high technical ability. As the narrator in *Les Martyres de Saint Sébastien*, which was written for her by the great poet, d'Annunzio, she found another ideal vehicle for her talent. Her static beauty lent grandeur to this declamatory role, with its scope for eurhythmic interpretation. The lavish pictorial ballets which she began producing with her own company were, however, generally disappointing. She tried to imitate the grand manner of Diaghilev, and had the means to commission work of the very great, such as Stravinsky and Ravel, but she lacked his daring and vision, and was too often inclined to centre the ballet on herself. Of her successes, many of which were largely attributable to the excellence of her collaborators, only Ravel's *Boléro* remains, and that thanks to Nijinska's curiously disturbing choreography. This was modified in later revivals by other companies. In this ballet the lone woman, dancing on an enormous and brightly lit table, centre stage, is surrounded by the turbulent desire of the men grouped around her in the shadow, giving a weird, pulsating effect of primitive desire in the final scene, when the chosen male jumps up and subdues the woman. The lush splendour of her production of Ravel's *La Valse* was so overwhelmingly rich that it completely obscured whatever dancing may have been present. She never learned the effective dignity of restraint, nor did she ever gauge the narrow limits of her own interpretative abilities. But her efforts remain remarkable as a symptom of that epoch.

---

[1] The archives were liquidated in 1952 by its eminent director, Pierre Tugal, who presented much valuable material to the Paris Opera Museum.

POST-WAR DEVELOPMENT

The post-war confusion in many spheres of life has been responsible for a splitting-up of the leading ballet companies and a re-distribution of talent. The pack of cards is being reshuffled, but the cards remain the same. The outstanding dancers of to-day are in the main those who made their reputations in the pre-war period, or whose budding talents were just unfolding. To-day promising newcomers appear one by one, as the older ones make their exits.

Several events had repercussions on the development of the dance. There was, for instance, the death of Fokine in New York in 1944. There was the banning of Serge Lifar from the Paris Opera Ballet in 1945. There was the exodus of foreign pupils from the famous Paris schools of Egorova, Preobrajenska and Volinine. There was the renaissance of French ballet with the sensational new group of the *Ballets des Champs Elysées* and the profound interest which the negro ballets of Berto Pasuko and Katherine Dunham created.

Many of the renowned classic dancers were in the United States during the war. Several have returned to the Continent. Paris remains as irresistible as ever. Balanchine and Nijinska have been commissioned to produce ballets for the Opera, and Toumanova considers it an honour to appear in them as guest artist. The artistic future of this venerable institution seems once more assured.

Adding to the present confusion caused by the amazing multiplicity of companies grouped round a few stars is the fact that modern ballet in America has produced new and interesting pieces, using both the modern dance and the classic technique. A good example of this is the work of Agnes de Mille, and her achievements in different fields are typical of a style which enriches ballet with contemporary influences and folk art. Her ballets for the Theatre Guild presentation of the musical play *Oklahoma* made her famous over-night. She used the dance not to create visual interludes, but to carry the significance of the plot further into dancing symbolism. In this way, the preparation of an unwilling bride becomes in the dance realization of all the subconscious fears of the virgin about to be sacrificed. In her Far-West ballet, *Rodeo*, in which she herself danced the central figure of the hobbledehoy but emotional cow-girl, she captures the spirit of the West in a way never before realized, bringing as true a national spirit to the dance as

Martha Graham did with her early-American pioneer-woman dances, which had more of drama then of ballet in them.

A famous company of New York is the Ballet Theatre, which brought together some of the best American dancers and choreographers, such as John Kriza, Jerome Robbins, and Michael Kidd. Robbin's sailor ballet, *Fancy Free*, has been hailed as a new departure in chamber ballet. Its young-American spirit is exemplified not only by the plot of sailors on a spree, but also by the incorporation of modern ballroom steps and of acrobatics in the ballet idiom.

This company produced Fokine's last work, *Bluebeard*, and also that most important contribution to the repertoire, Antony Tudor's *Pillar of Fire*. The lasting success of this work established the fame of this young British choreographer. The group was furthermore fortunate in having two outstanding American ballerinas: Nora Kaye and Rosella Hightower.

The Russians sojourning in America split up into the *Ballets Russes*, and Colonel de Basil's *Original Ballet Russe*. Between them they shared the old ballet repertoire, and the dancers of pre-war fame: Danilova, Verchinina, Eglevsky, Jasinsky, etc. Famous couples such as Baronova-Massine, Riabouchinska-Lichine, and Markova-Dolin appeared from time to time in various companies as guest artists. Massine's first full-length ballet film on a tale of Andersen, 'The Red Shoes' revealed the great possibilities of this medium as well as the film talents of the beautiful Scotch redhead of the Covent Garden Ballet, Moira Shearer. After a less succesful 'Tales of Hoffman' Hollywood had started with an entire series of ballet films, directed by such vastly different choreographer-dancers as Gene Kelly and Roland Petit, including the much discussed project of a life of Pavlova, in which the mannered but beautiful Toumanova would incarnate the Immortal One.

The Sadler's Wells company of London is now Britain's real national ballet, still under the valiant direction of Ninette de Valois. The tremendous encouragement the public gave to it, even during the darkest years of the war, has born fruit. To-day the company has two groups, of which the most spectacular is the ballet at Covent Garden. Works by Frederick Ashton and Robert Helpmann, who are among the foremost in their profession, are greatly enhanced by the interpretations of an outstanding cast. Margot Fonteyn has developed from a pupil at Sadler's Wells to one of the outstanding ballerinas of the world to-day. The fact that the Covent Garden company can present *Giselle* with three dancers performing the title role in turn, each worthy in her own right to claim the part, speaks for itself. If Fonteyn's Giselle is supreme, Moira Shearer and Beryl Grey can certainly hold their own in this most exacting part, which calls for an actress as well as a dancer. Other dancers who have progressed steadily to full maturity are Violetta Elvin, Alexander Grant and Brian Shaw.

Marie Rambert's chamber ballet has grown from a modest beginning into a more important group. Since 1926, when she presented her first programme of English ballet, she has gone far. She schooled important choreographers, such as Frederick Ashton, Antony Tudor and Andrée Howard, and her present repertoire includes the most important of their works. Of her dancer-choreographers Walter Gore and David Paltenghi have recently contributed the most to her repertoire. Modern classics of her repertoire were Andrée Howard's powerful 'Lady into Fox', based on David Garnet's novel, and the full-length dance story 'Sailor's Return', another important contribution to national British ballet. Both ballets were interpreted to perfection by one of Rambert's outstanding pupils, who for years was her leading dancer, Sally Gilmour. Miss Howard, incidently, had to wait until 1952 to get the highest official consacration of her talent in Great Britain, when Dame Ninette de Valois commissioned a ballet for the Covent Garden company, 'A Mirror for Witches', a haunting story of witchcraft set in the New England of the last century.

Of Rambert's later presentations a highly intellectual ballet of David Paltenghi stands out: 'Canterbury Tales' a mediæval affair inspired by Chaucer's immortal work, with music by a significant young English composer Peter Racine Fricker.

Of Tudor's many works first tried out in Rambert's own pocket-size Mercury Theatre in London, she still gives refreshingly charming performances of 'Soirée Musicale', 'Gala Performance' and that lyrical classic 'Lilac Garden'.

In France since the end of the second World War, a young company of outstanding brilliance has been formed. This Ballets des Champs Elysées has a future. It is headed by Boris Kochno and the dancer-choreographer, Roland Petit. Their young dancers, Jean Babilée (whose elevation is remarkable) and Irène Skorik, seem destined to become famous. The lovely French-Spanish ballerina, Anna Nevada, and the former Opera-ballet star, Solange Schwarz, form, together with choreographer Janine Charrat, a powerful trio of imaginative interpreters. The latter created Stravinsky's ballet, *Jeu de Cartes*. The celebrated painter, Marie Laurencin, whose *décor* for Poulenc's *Les Biches* has survived from the Diaghilev days, has surpassed herself in *Le Déjeuner sur l' Herbe*, with its delightful old-world music by Joseph Lanner. Another creation of importance is the Jean Cocteau dance poem, *Le Jeune Homme et la Mort*, to music by Bach, with Petit as choreographer. There are only two interpreters in this ballet, Jean Babilée and Nathalie Philippart. These two artists had given a very personal touch to their dancing of *Spectre de la Rose*. As a team they scored a further success with this totally different but highly theatrical theme, which only that strange genius of the theatre, Cocteau, could have developed. His astonishing gift for lyrical transformation, very apparent in the great play, *The Eagle has Two Heads*, which he wrote at the same time as this little dance-drama, gives an infinitely poetic quality to this ballet. It is also an important example of intimate collaboration between author and choreographer.

Immediately after the war Serge Lifar was the principal dancer of the New Ballet de Monte Carlo. His new choreographies with this company include *Salomé*, arranged from the opera by Richard Strauss, and the more important ballet, *Dramme per Musica*, arranged to a secular cantata by Bach. There is little dramatic action. The sequence of dances might, according to Cyril Beaumont, be called 'studies in choreographic architecture'. Yvette Chauviré was the company's leading ballerina, and showed as much brillian-ce as she did in the film of the Paris opera ballet, *La Mort du Cygne*, which first brought her to the fore, in pre-war days.

It is said that the standard of classic ballet in Russia to-day is as high as ever. A few dancers, who have been allowed outside the country for guest appearances, have confirmed this impression. Marina Semenova and Assaf Messerer were seen in Paris before the war. Their technique, as well as Messerer's gift for choreography, was remarkable. Galina Ulanova received the high honour of the Stalin Prize in 1945. Of the Soviet ballets seen outside Russia, only *The Red Poppy* could hold its own as a work of the first rank. Its theme, however, was pure propaganda. Shostakovitch's *The Golden Age* and some of Prokofiev's new music are considered vital contributions to modern ballet music. Another feature of new Soviet ballet is its use of varied forms of national folk-lore, not only to preserve folk-dancing but also to use it for the expression of new emotions through the traditional steps. Formerly, ballet used Spanish, Hungarian and Polish folk-dances. Now the stronger rhythms and exotic flavour of Georgian and Ukrainian dances are introduced.

For instance, the strong male battle-dance, *The Heart of The Hills*, with a dramatic choreography by another of Russia's new male stars, Vakhtang Chabukiani, shows this trend. It is of interest to note that Russia now possesses official critics and historians of the dance, whose works so far are not available to the European public. In years to come, however, the names of Yuri Slonimsky and Vladimar Potapov may become significant to balletomanes.

National ballet flourishes in several other countries. The Royal Opera of Copenhagen, with its long ballet tradition, established by Auguste Bournonville, maintains the national style with classic folk-ballets. Prague has re-staged some new Czecho-Slovakian ballets, and in Germany the ballet group of the Staatsoper revived *Petrouchka*, Gluck's *Don Juan*, and Prokofiev's *Romeo and Juliet*. In Holland the National Wagner Ballet was deprived of its competent ballet-mistress, Yvonne Georgi, a Wigman pupil, who reverted to classic ballet. The years of the German occupation saw the creation of such interesting works as *Les Animaux Modèles*, Poulenc's latest ballet, and the mediæval theme, *Carmina Burata*, performed to music by Carl Orff. This ballet was partly inspired by Gregorian chants. The use of choirs of nuns and monks on the stage, taking part in the action, was novel and effective. At present she continues this work with the Düsseldorf opera ballet. In Portugal the folk-dancers, Ruth and Francis Graca, took over the ballet of the Lisbon opera, re-organised and raised its standard considerably. In their latest creations they introduced national themes and national music. The *conquistadores* ballet, *Verde Gayos*, is reported to be the most significant to date.

In Australia a new tradition was built up by Hélène Kirsova, who had settled down there after her warm reception as a soloist of the de Basil Ballet. Founding the first ballet-school in the country based entirely on the great classic tradition, she managed to present her own company within the year, though at the time many of the leading roles were danced by the few Russian artists who had remained in the country after the outbreak of war in Europe. During the subsequent war years she definitely established her own style of choreography, of which the three-act ballet, *Faust*, and the five-act one, *Revolution of the Umbrellas*, both with special music by Henry Krips, were individual successes. Of the dancers she trained, Peggy Sager, Rachel Cameron, and Henry Legerton may climb to the top of their profession. Loudon Sainthill proved himself to be a stage designer with a clear grasp of the special problems and requirements of ballet *décor*. Other painters employed were Amy Kingston and Wolfgang Cardamatis.

The good work was continued by Edouard Borovansky, another soloist of de Basil's ballet, who had established himself in Australia. In the beginning he gave small-scale ballets, and later his own versions of *Swan Lake*, *Coppelia* and *Scheherazade*. His company was enlarged with pupils and solo dancers of the Kirsova ballet, with Tamara Tchinarova heading the cast. He presented a ballet with a national flavour, *Terra Australis*, and other original ballets introducing young Australian dancers. In William Constable he has found a talented designer of costumes and decor. A few of the pupils Borovansky trained went overseas to acquire international repute. Kathleen Gorham became solodancer with the Sadlers Wells Theatre Ballet, Dorothy Stephenson choreographer with International Ballet, Boris Trunoff leading dancer with Dolin. These dancers, and occasional guest artists of the standard of Poul Gnatt of the Danish Royal Ballet, return to the country for a few seasons, to keep the standard of this young company of a young country astoundingly high. Of recent Borovansky choreographies a honorable failure of Australian folklore flavour must be mentioned: '*The capture of Ned Kelly*', a gangster of the goldrush days resuscitated in an unsuitable ballet idiom with expressionist leanings. Other more poetic legends, such as '*The Black Swan*', telling of the discovery of the new country by Dutch explorers in a purely romantic vein, are much more in the choreographers line. Production of the full-length '*Sleeping Beauty*' was another important feat.

Second official company is the Melbourne National Ballet, which developed under the artistic direction of Joyce Graeme and Rex Reid, dancers from the Rambert Ballet. Later Walter Gore and his wife Paula Hinton took over for some time. They achieved most creditable performances of an exacting work, the entire 'Swanlake', which revealed a decor designer of promise, Ann Church, and a ballerina of unusual stamina Lynn Golding, who danced the exacting dual role of Odette-Odile night after night.

More important perhaps was the creation by the young company of an Australian ballet, presented in aboriginal masks, called 'Corroboree', on the magnificent score of John Antill, with a careful and clever choreography of Australian Rex Reid, who had adapted the anthropological documents of the authentic dances of the blacks to the balletic idiom. Almost abstract in its sequence of seven dance suites (Dance of the Frog Totem,

25. George Zorich as the Moor, Rosella Hightower as the Doll, and Serge Golovine in the title role of 'Petrouchka' with the Marquis de Cuevas Ballet

26. Maria Tallchief and Francisco Moncion dance the 'Firebird' with the New York City Ballet

27.   Alicia Alonso and John Kriza with Ballet Theatre in the American saga 'Billy the Kid'

28. Agnes de Mille in her own ballet, 'Rodeo'

29. The Cuevas Ballet presents a striking Skibine choreography 'The Prisoner of the Caucasus',
with Rosella Hightower and George Skibine

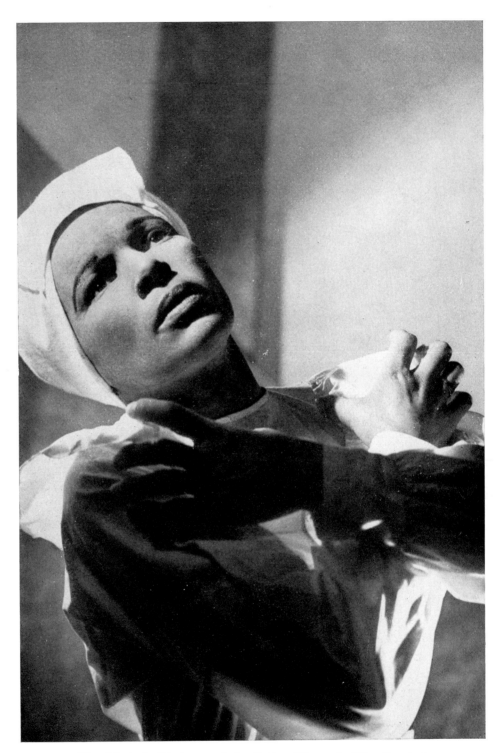

30. Marjorie Blackman of the Ballets Nègres in 'The Prophet'

31. Berto Pasuko, choreographer of the Ballets Nègres, in 'They came'

32. Russian Folkdance—Bodenwieser Dance Group

33. Janine Charrat in Beethoven's VIIth Symphony

34.   Hélène Kirsova in Col. de Basil's production of 'Carnaval'

35. Rachel Cameron and Philippe Perrottet, of the Melbourne Ballet Society, in aboriginal dance legend, 'Arckaringa'

36. The Kirsova Ballet creates 'Faust' with Tamara Tchinarova and Henry Legerton

Rain Ceremony, Procession of the Firesticks, etc.) it was always fully satisfying as a dance spectacle, which kept enough of the original primitive flavour to make it seem authentic.

Of the few small-scale companies the creative one of Laurel Martyn—herself possibly the best Australian Giselle—stands out. Of my own small touring-group of the 'Sydney Dancers' I will write in a later chapter.

CHAPTER SIX

REVOLUTION IN THE DANCE WORLD

Dancing provides a dual means of satisfying the longing
for a sense of group fellowship, and the wish of the indivi-
dual to display himself to fullest advantage
Havelock Ellis

GREEK DANCING AND EURHYTHMICS

THE revolt against the mannerisms and the artificiality of the classic ballet, which at the beginning of this century found itself at its lowest artistic ebb, was led by Isadora Duncan. She proclaimed the liberation of all art from its 'civilized bonds', and went back to ancient Greece as a source for her inspiration. It was her avowed aim to destroy ballet as a disciplined dance form, completely alien to her undisciplined spirit.

She won half of the battle through her undoubted personal charm and sincerity. When she appeared with her pupils they formed a background of movement for the fervent and inspired priestess, Isadora. She danced on the sacred hill of the Acropolis, emulating the style of the ancient chorus, but in a markedly personal manner. With the puerile simplicity of pseudo-Hellenic doctrines, with a displaced mysticism and a muddled pagan philosophy, she confused the issue. It would have been better if she had been satisfied to remain the solo-dancer of grace and originality, instead of becoming an ardent propagandist for a new form of living. She repudiated the classical alphabet of dancing, which she had never mastered herself, and gaining disciples galore, she opened the theatre to the dilettante and the many indifferent Duncan imitators. She was well over forty, and still dancing, when a motor accident on the Riviera caused her sudden and tragic death. As a stout woman, approaching middle age, she danced Tchaikovsky's Fifth Symphony in flaming, revolutionary red in Soviet Russia, to the pained surprise of even her staunchest admirers.

Her brother, Raymond Duncan, the eccentric poet-weaver, and her niece, the dancer, Lisa Duncan, carried on her principles in Paris and New York, giving dreary exhibitions of *The Duncan Dancers*. One should rather say that they preserved these dances as museum pieces, of documentary interest only.

Isadora Duncan undoubtedly influenced Fokine when she gave her recitals in St. Petersburg in 1907, which were enthusiastically received. Through Fokine she waged the battle against formal and too rigid classicism which, in a later period Massine won with the easy victory of his masterpieces. But another most important influence was universally felt, the doctrine of Jacques Dalcroze, the Swiss musician. He introduced, in that same epoch before the first World War, his system of eurhythmic movement.

This system was intended to develop the musical sense of the pupil through harmonious gymnastics and bodily awareness. It gained enormous prestige, and many dancers benefited by it because it greatly developed musical and rhythmical feeling. Dalcroze himself used movement only as a means of being aware of rhythm and musical metre, not to interpret its moods. He never intended to make stage presentations of his group exercises; in fact, he was violently opposed to this. Many of his followers, however, adapted his principles to a 'free dance' of their own invention, using the bare feet and the draped tunics in what was then known as the Duncan style.

THE CENTRAL-EUROPEAN SCHOOLS

Rudolph von Laban, pupil of Dalcroze, was the first dancer and teacher to form an expressionist dance group, in Northern Germany, giving stage interpretations of what he called the plastic dance. Thus, out of the blue, the German school of free-movement dancing was born.

A study of their first teaching of basic principles reveals the denial of every detail of classic tradition and discipline. They prided themselves on not having any roots in the culture of the past. They did, however, have a vague leaning towards the exotic. Laban must have been impressed by the rather doubtful Oriental dancers of his day, Sent M'Ahesa and the 'Javanese temple dancer', Mata Hari, who was better known in another field.

They advocated plastic pantomime surcharged with emotion, which encouraged the weird and the neurotic, anything to be 'different'. Though the spectacle might be interesting when seen for the first time, the approach to the real art of dancing was only spasmodic, and ballet, in as far as it should be the illustration and interpretation of a musical work, was disparaged.

The most gifted colleague of von Laban was Mary Wigman, who later on started her famous school in Munich, out of which, through the coming of the Nazi regime, the school of Günther developed. From Munich the gospel spread through Central Europe and the best pupils of Wigman founded schools of their own. Gertrud Leistikov became the exponent of the free art in Holland. The sisters Wiesenthal, the 'Queens of the Waltz', opened a school in Vienna. Rose Chladek was the only one who tried to propagate this creed in the Latin countries, where, however, it has never been taken seriously.

What the pupils lacked in technique was made up in their abundance of enthusiasm. The doors of these schools were opened wide to all sorts of eager girls, whose amateurish efforts were often more enhanced by physical charm then by real skill in dancing. The fact that any young and pretty girl, moving gracefully to engaging music, has a certain appeal, helped greatly. Charlotte Bara, Lili Green, Niddy Impekoven—these are only a few of the names which were acclaimed by the public at the time.

Wigman personally has shown us some interesting and original dancing, even though it was always too angular, too heavy, and too intense. She failed in her direction of her group, though she herself fondly thought that her 'architectural and geometrical structure' of mass movements was supreme. Her work, and that of her pupils, suffered from two fundamental weaknesses: the connection between the dancing and the music was always obscure, if not non-existent, and the new technique, being in any case a haphazard discovery, did not give a sound basis of movement.

When examining the free movements of the Wigman system in detail, one discovers a typical substitution of elbow for arm movements. These are used to express energy, but their expression becomes soon strained and highly unnatural through much repetition. The critic, Haskell, called it wittily 'the school of the clenched fist and the flat feet.'

The position of the feet, turned out to an exaggerated degree flat on the floor, exemplifies this statement. Wigman maintained that this position was necessary in order to acquire elasticity in jumping. Yet she herself had no elevation to speak of, and the classic school, with its stress on elevation, for the male dancers in particular, shows conclusively that this ugly out-turned position of the bent knees is unnecessary.

There are always endless ways of enriching choreography, if one wants to enlarge the scope of this medium of interpretation. The daring innovations of solo movements and group handling of Fokine, Massine and Nijinska have shown this conclusively. Many avenues have been explored, and many more await discovery. This pioneering work, however, necessitates a foundation of basic knowledge.

37. Shona Dunlop and Emmy Taussig, of the Bodenwieser Group, in a study of moods

38. Darja Collin, former choreographer of the Amsterdam Opera Ballet, in 'Galop' of Casella

39. Her partner, Edmée Monod, in Poulenc's 'Pastourelle'

40. The expressionist danceteam, Evelyn Ippen and Bettina Vernon, in 'Conscience'

41. Amsterdam Opera Ballet in 'Orpheus and Eurydice', composed by Henk Badings

42.   Ted Shawn, in one of his religious dances, as Saint Francis

43. A study in Eurhythmics, with Shona Dunlop and Hilary Napier

44. Portuguese Folk Ballet, with Ruth and Francis Graça

Although she lacked this, Wigman dared to explore hitherto unknown by-paths, with the result that her excursions into the realm of the nightmare, the frenzy and the neurotic—mistakenly called ecstatic, visionary and religious—were unbalanced. When Wigman lashed herself into a fury, a dervish dance of interest might be the result, but any beauty it possessed was purely coincidental. One never could see those dances twice without being bored, whereas in the classic ballet a different rendering by other interpreters of the same part may cause infinite pleasure.

The reason for the immense popularity of the Central-European School in their own stricken and humiliated territories can, perhaps, be explained psychologically. At the time of the School's foundation any movement of open social revolt was difficult, but as artistic revolt could not be forbidden it found its outlet in the dance. And what could be emotionally more satisfying than a rebellion against the century-old dictatorship of the French-Italian-Russian academies of dancing, which inferred that they alone were able to keep the torch of culture burning?

It was therefore quite logical for this movement to start in the Germany of that period. It provided a natural outlet for a long-suffering youth, which was beset by inhibitions, complexes and neuroses, in fact by all the convenient afflictions which Freud was then obligingly explaining to them in detail.

THE SURVIVORS

The expressionist dance group of the Kurt Jooss Ballet, as it calls itself, is probably the best-trained exponent of the modern dance-drama. It certainly is most solidly established and has gained public favour in Europe and in the United States. Its productions are most homogeneous, as a result of long years of working together, interrrupted by the war, but now once more continued on the old footing.

Kurt Jooss himself was never a prominent dancer. He studied with Mary Wigman and he was later, before the advent of Naziism, ballet-master at the Düsseldorf Opera House. His group won European recognition and first prize in an international dance competition held in Paris in 1932. They then made their headquarters at Dartington Hall, in England, and during the recent war a depleted company gave performances in America. They have now returned to their original home in Essen, Germany, once more ready to continue, undaunted and imperturbable, to travel the world.

To-day Kurt Jooss is still the outstanding choreographer of the modern dance-drama, even though his latest efforts show monotonous repetition and seem variations of his earlier work. His structure is generally sound and comprehensive, and in this he differs from his teacher, Wigman, who could never handle groups satisfactorily. His compositions, however, seem to lack the logic of the classics, and certainly their poetic atmosphere and charm. He made up for these short-comings with the originality of his themes, often based on the happenings of everyday life, which he deftly transposed to the stage. He scorned neither political implications nor social satire.

His earliest creations remain the best. One of these is also a musical find—Ravel's *Pavane pour un Infante défunt*, with its excellent depiction of Spanish Court life and its stateliness in the manner of Velasquez. There is his *Big City*, in which the hackneyed theme is saved from banality by his deft handling of groups, creating the atmosphere of a busy and perverted metropolis. In it he portrays the factory girl and her poor lover, the rich man-about-town, virtue betrayed and wickedness recompensed, as it is so often in real life. In the crazy speed of the opening scene—telegraph boys, street arabs, prostitutes, policemen and idle drunkards—there is mechanical motion, suppressed excitement, rhythm, tempo, and poignancy of emotion. Such a scene is more easily expressed through his chosen medium of free movement and mime than could, perhaps, have been the case with a more severely controlled classic treatment. It was akin, somehow, in its tragic intensity, to Helpmann's *Miracle in the Gorbals* and to one of the first ballets of the Champs Elysées company, *Le Rendez-vous*, with the 'children of the people embracing, leaning against the doors of the night...'

The choreography of Jooss carries within itself the germ of its own destruction. Its unorthodox nature must in this case eventually lead it to the point where too much freedom of movement means the end of discipline and co-ordination. He is a dictator who expects automatic reactions from his dancers, with the result that their personalities are cramped. Excellent mimics as most of them are, they adhere strictly to the character parts allotted to them, but somehow they do not seem to rise above the part. It may seem a paradox, but it is a fact that free movement in this style of work means the suppression of the dancer's individuality.

It leads to nowhere, despite all its cleverness and originality, and even despite the sharp satire on diplomats in that outstanding work, *The Green*

Table, which, by gaining him the first prize in Paris, put Jooss on his feet in the world of international art.

Some of the soloists who originally helped to establish the reputation of the group are still with it after its post-war re-organization. The character dancer, Elsa Kahle, the graceful Noëlle de Mosa, who is of Dutch extraction, and Hans Zulig, head the cast, the latter also working as choreographer. They still suffer from an apparently inherent lack of a true sense of music. In fact, the musical potpourris of the great composers which Jooss uses for his ballets have never been quite happy. Nor has the music written specially for him, and habitually executed on two pianos, been very remarkable. The music for *The Green Table*, by his old collaborator, Fritz Cohen, was merely effective but not of lasting significance.

Another expressionist group, that of Gertrud Bodenwieser, of Vienna, became first known by gaining the second prize in that same Paris competition of 1932. The work was an original study in rhythmics, called *The Machine Age*. The ballet-mistress, who had set out as one of the first teachers of the dance at the State Conservatorium of Vienna, took her group of girls all over the world. Just before the outbreak of war in Europe they established themselves in Australia, where for the first time they introduced the free style.

A grave short-coming of the group, most seriously felt in their major dance dramatisation, *Oh! World*, is the absence of adequate male dancers. Some of the girls specialize in the never quite satisfying travesty dancing of the male parts. In a varied repertoire, relying partly on the use of stage effects and partly on the undeniable glamour of the girls, the artistic integrity suffers, even though the spectacle as a whole is pleasantly entertaining. Shona Dunlop is an excellent character dancer, and the Czecho-Slovakian pair, Evelyn Ippen and Bettina Vernon, who were of the original group, have distinguished themselves as solo dancers of the expressionist type.

Though the Central-European Schools attack ballet as being stilted and obsolete, it appears that their own style is unable to rejuvenate itself sufficiently to avoid monotony and repetition. It has become static and may, in its turn, become obsolete. But this modern school has to be self-sufficient, of necessity if not by choice. The classic ballet-master can admire, learn, and adapt new ideas of the free-movement school to his own work, but the free-movement choreographer cannot so easily draw on the classics, because the method is devoid of classic technique. There seems no way out of this impasse.

It is to be hoped that in the near future the interesting modern American school of 'dance drama' will make its influence felt in Europe. So far only the group of Graham has been seen and admired in several countries, but its inspiring influence has only manifested itself in timid imitations of a few solodancers. And, even though imitation is the sincerest form of flattery, this is not enough. The innovations of many of the American moderns should be digested, rather than adapted, merged with the original Central-European style, in order that on both sides of the Ocean a new kind of dance drama may develop, suited to the different temperaments, each one going its own way.

Anyway, the Europeans of the 'modern style' have by now accepted the necessity of rigid training from early childhood, akin to the schooling needed for ballet, in order to make body and mind pliable enough to realise all the intentions and all the experiments of the choreographer. Once the classic technique has been mastered, it is time enough to turn away and attempt to discover other paths, which will lead to more original... perhaps more contemporary... expression. But in order to be able to do this, the academic training from an early age seems imperative.

CHAPTER SEVEN

STAGE DANCING OF OCCIDENT AND ORIENT

All well-bred men should have mastered the art of singing and dancing
Plato

No man dances when sober
Cicero

THE EUROPEANS

FOLLOWERS of the Central-European 'free' style have influenced several smaller groups, representing remote countries. In most cases, however, this stage influence has been used carefully and sparingly, as in the admirable Spanish company of 'Coros y Danzas', and in the Yugoslavian Dance Group.

They take their inspiration mainly from the national dance sources. Many of these dances, made ready for stage presentation, have been piously put together again by a research choreographer, thus preserving many ancient folkart forms from threatening extinction. The work of these semi-professional and amateur groups are most important in present-day dance development.

There also exist professional dance personalities, who are difficult to define, yet merit their place in history. The modern school of French mime has certainly helped the great actor-producer Jean Louis Barrault to master his stage craft and to be at the same time a dancer worthy of the commedia dell'arte... yet some of his pupils, who give mime recitals cannot be called dancers in the accepted sense of the word.

A mime-dancer such as Marcel Marceau obviously comes directly from this French school, a grotesque dancer as Cilly Wang from the German one... yet, though their art borders sometimes on the music-hall performance, they manage to convey something entirely their own. Clotilde and Alexander Sakharoff were sensational 'modern' dancers after the first worldwar... today in their maturity they still continue, although they have wandered far from their original 'Laban' style. Harald Kreutzberg, most outspokenly a product of the German school, has remained more himself... and he still is the greatest of them all, undefeated by approaching middle age. Sometimes he masters his body with an almost acrobatic facility... then again he knows how to conjure up images and moods with a single flick of the finger. With a crown on his bald head he is the legendary noble king... a moment later he wears a motoring cap to become every inch the little man in the street, the student, or the lover.

Again escaping exact classification there are the individual solo dancers who need a group of their own to realise their strictly non-balletic intentions for their 'dance stories'.

There are the Viennese queens of the waltz, the Wiesenthal sisters, who have formed several generations of Viennese dance groups.

The Swiss dancer, Trudy Schoop, and her group have brought us quite a new form of dance pantomime in an expressionist vein. All her dance stories were frankly directed towards the presentation of herself as a star, and the exploitation of her unusual and highly individual medium. In classifying her inimitable style we might call her the 'satirist of the modern dance', although she goes in for much more than mere caricatures such as formed the stock in trade of a few grotesque dancers preceding her, particularly the German solo dancer, Valeska Gert.

Trudy Schoop, as a mime, has been compared with Charlie Chaplin. Even physically this mere wisp of a girl reminds one of this great veteran of the screen. With her round eyes and straggling hair, she is as convincing an Orphan Annie as one could encounter on any stage, but an Orphan Annie with her tongue in her cheek.

She established her name in Central Europe with her two-act ballet, *Fridolin*. In this pantomime-dance the legendary type of the naughty little Teutonic schoolboy, with his funny little round hat, was most wittily portrayed. Fridolin's various adventures were subtly mimed with great speed and precision, which exhibited Schoop's classical training and acrobatic abilities to perfection. Although she used these sparingly and soberly, these slick dancing scenes, even with their perfect timing, were studded with too many trick effects, and savoured more of the music hall than of a dance recital.

Their great weakness lay in the choice of their music, as was so often the case with Kurt Jooss and other exponents of the expressionist art. Their dances were performed to unimportant modern compositions, which were in most cases written especially for them by the accompanist, long after the general outline of the dance had been determined.

Trudy Schoop's outstanding pre-war success was the three-act dance play, *All for love (Alles aus Liebe)*, in which she succeeded in presenting herself, supported by a small but excellent company of Swiss mimes, in a dance tale which ran through the entire evening, and whose plot held the audience as much in suspense as if it had been a thriller.

This type of venture is always perilous, yet it has been attempted in ballet now and again. Seventeenth century France saw *divertissements* which ran throughout the entire evening, and Tchaikovsky attempted it with his four-act ballet, *Sleeping Beauty*. This was presented in its entirety by Diaghilev in London in 1921 with disastrous results, causing its re-arrangement into the one-act ballet, *Aurora's Wedding*. Hélène Kirsova, with her Australian company, also created a three-act ballet, *Faust*, which remains one of her best

Trudy Schoop's *All for Love* shows, in a sequence of scenes, the adventures of a little housemaid, first discovered in the arms of her employer's son, promptly sacked and tramping the streets in search of another job. She is a servant girl in a typical German beer garden, later assistant in an exclusive hairdresser's salon, then the model of a cubist painter. A scene in which the enthusiastic art snobs visit the exhibition and glare and goggle in front of absolutely empty frames, or the portrayal of a second-rate ladies' orchestra at a charity show, are masterpieces of subtle wit. It is all most diverting, but it might become a little tiring and puerile, were it not for the gifted and tragi-comic personality of Trudy Schoop herself.

Her style is inimitable and consequently has no chance of survival. This is fundamentally a one-woman show, excellent though the supporting cast may be. It is an accident, and a happy one, rather than a development.

In Holland, Gertrud Leistikov and Lili Green spread the Wigman cult. In 1930 or thereabouts another well-known Wigman pupil, Yvonne Georgi, who formerly had been Harald Kreutzberg's partner, founded what was euphemistically called the 'National Wagner Ballet'. It was part of the private Wagner Society which had the famous Concertgebouw orchestra at its disposal, and which sponsored guest performances in Holland by such great companies as the Berlin State Opera and the Paris Opera.

Georgi exhibited a marked expressionist style in the beginning, but she later reverted partly to the classic ballet. Her productions provided an outlet for modern Dutch composers such as Henk Badings and Willem Pyper, and for the advanced school of Dutch painters. She gained some measure of success with her simplified versions of *Coppelia* and Purcell's *Festive Dances*, but she failed when trying to interpret a more exacting theme such as the allegoric *Diana* or *Orpheus and Eurydice*.

After the war, when the Dutch National Opera Ballet was reorganised the charming solodancer Darja Collin took over but she failed both as balletmistress and choreographer.

While Yvonne Georgi went back to her native Germany to restage some of her significant Amsterdam successes in Düsseldorf, the ballet came under the wholesome influence of one of Lifar's assistants, the choreographer, Françoise Adret.

With the stress once again laid upon the classic school two of Holland's best ballet dancers, Mascha Stom and Pieter van der Sloot, came into their own.

In Germany the schools of von Laban and Wigman died a natural death. With the coming of the Nazis the school of Günther carried on, but it did not progress or evolve any new ideas. The gong and the drum, the coloured tunics and the outstretched arm were still the order of the day. They were chosen to represent Germany officially in Paris, together with Harold Kreutzberg, and with the ballet group of the Berlin State Opera, in the International Dance Festival of 1938.

COMBINATION OF BALLET AND FOLK-DANCE

On the borders of the expressionist domain lie those national dance groups which have presented ballets inspired by native dancing while, at the same time, being strongly influenced by the expressionist school.

Dance groups of this nature have worked in Spain, in Italy and in Portugal. In Italy the high level of technique has been maintained, but the creation of ballet has come to a standstill. Neither at the Scala in Milan, nor at the Opera in Rome have they contributed much to the modernization of opera ballet, and the choreographies given in their own right, even when coloured by elements of the national dance, have been unimportant.

The Portuguese folk-ballet of Francis and Ruth Graça has been mentioned elsewhere. The woman, only Portuguese by marriage, was trained in Central Europe. Consequently it is no wonder that their productions in Lisbon show strong expressionist tendencies.

In Spain the dance situation is of particular interest. A century or so ago romantic ballet flourished in Madrid, and had a decidedly national colour. Folk-dances like the *Bolero* and the *Zapateado* were done with castanets and *sur les pointes*. Some of the ballerinas abroad, particularly Fanny Elssler and

45. The Swiss mime, Trudy Schoop, and her company, in the circusparody 'That's Barbara'

46. The Schoop company in the three-act dance, 'Blonde Marie'

47. Ted Shawn in a Japanese sword dance

48. Ram Gopal and Shurita in a dance of the Bharata Natya style of Southern India

49. Ram Gopal as the God Indra in a Hindu dance legend

50. Hindu Mudras: The opening of a Lotus flower (hands of Indradev Prasad)

51.   Indradev Prasad in 'Invocation'

52.   Annamite dance legend, with Janine Charrat and Indo-Chinese company

later Lola Montez, adventuress and Royal mistress rather than ballet-dancer, affected this Spanish style. The decline of ballet in general throughout the world in the second half of the last century, has been prolonged in Spain until our day. The fame of Spanish dancing abroad was entirely founded on the success of the folk-dances of Andalusia.

One of the best ballets of Massine, on a score of de Falla, was *The Three-cornered Hat*, in which authentic forms of folk-dancing were given within the frame of ballet. Diaghilev, in his heyday, also presented a *Cuadro Flamenco* produced as a gipsy ballet, for which native stars such as La Faraona and Pastora Imperio were engaged. Juan Gris and Pablo Picasso contributed the *décor* for these ballets, accentuating their Andalusian atmosphere.

La Argentina, at the peak of her European fame, attempted to revive Spanish ballet during one season at the Théatre Fémina in Paris. She astounded with the vigour of de Falla's gipsy ballet, *Love the Magician* (*El Amor Brujo*), with its weird fire dance. Another great Spanish dancer of pre-war fame, Vicente Escudero, repeated the attempt. His rather feeble efforts to co-ordinate authentic Spanish movements with a group dance in the German style spoiled the effect. To-day ballet in Spain struggles only feebly to survive.

Main local ballet tradition is kept up in Barcelona, with the opera ballet of the Lyceo. The true Spanish dance art, however, has gained tremendously in prestige since the end of the Civil War in Spain (1939).

Folkdancing is officially encouraged in all provinces. Yearly competitions are held and the winners of each group are sometimes send abroad to give proof of the living tradition of the old lore. The 'Danzas y Coros de España', combining some twenty provincial groups, totalling hundred and fifty artists of semi-professional status but of a high standard in their own regional art, have been touring Europe and some have gone as far afield as the two Americas.

The authentic Spanish folkdance as well as the Gitano style, the Flamenco dance, is so eminently theatrical that it is obvious why Spanish dancing, once it gained recognition abroad, would continue to be increasingly popular with world audiences. Today, indeed, we see an unprecedented boom of this art, as represented by a score of smaller and larger touring companies, headed of course by that very great dancer, the 'Nijinsky of Spain' Antonio, and his charming childhood partner Rosario. We will deal with these artists in a separate chapter.

INFLUENCE ON ORIENTAL DANCERS

Several Hindu dance groups invaded the Western world, and met with extraordinary success. Some of these artists remained for long years in the Occident, and were influenced by the expressionist style. Dramatizing their effects, they strengthened the appeal of their art for an occidental public, but detracted naturally from its authenticity and its age-old tradition.

There is a fundamental difference between occidental and oriental dancing. No classic technique can be as severe as the stylization of oriental dance movements, whose sacred origin and meaning are always apparent. In the Orient to-day there still exist complete royal ballet groups, formed by a ruler and kept for his exclusive entertainment. The sacred temple dancers of antiquity who dedicated their lives to the holy dance cult are soul-sisters of these frail, gorgeously adorned virgins, who enter the service of their king, the descendant of the gods, and who are his, body and soul.

The dancers of the royal Cambodian and the Javanese ballets, as well as of the more plebeian village ballets of Bali, dance historical legends and myths. They incarnate mythical figures of the Hindu *Rhamajana* legends and mime in the conventional *muðra* language with the aid of five hundred different gestures and positions of the hands and arms. They do not exteriorize as our dancers do. Their movements always centre round their own bodies, and each gesture performs an arc which returns to the body. They are static rather than dynamic dancers, conscious of the sacred meaning of their art, which is like a religious rite. They seem to be propelled across the stage by a rhythm of their own, and a mysterious inner volition, which is independent of the music, makes them appear as if they were possessed by the sacred spirits.

This impression can be only given when the dances are most authentic, and in those instances the possession of the spirit does actually take place, which occasions trance dances in a hypnotized and somnambulistic state. Needless to say that those dances have to be witnessed in their proper native surroundings. They were first shown in all their authenticity by the ballet group of Bali which travelled to the colonial exhibition of Paris in 1931. The *bari* dances of the warriors and the *legong* dances of the virgins, supremely beautiful, created a sensation. But the kris dances and the trance dances of the *legongs* were naturally absent from these stage performances.

The German schools borrowed, as we have mentioned elsewhere, the most effective gestures of these exotic dances. On the other hand, most of the oriental dancers, who came to Europe when the vogue for this style of little-known dancing started, were in their turn influenced by the Central-European schools, and incorporated some of its flowing free movement in their own stage compositions.

This led in some instances to a weakening of the effect because all the charm of the authentic stylization had gone. A typical example is found in the work of Raden Mas Jodjana, the aristocratic dancer from the Court of Djocjacarta in Java, who came to the West and married a European wo-man. His Court and temple dances, once pure in style, deteriorated. He opened a school in the Pyrenees, in which he taught a mixture of Balinese and Javanese movements, greatly modified by the expressionist style. In this way he arrived, like so many others, at good stage effects which might, with the same chance of success, be executed by Europeans.

As a result several of the expressionist dancers, who in the first instance had learned the easy oriental effects of the Wigman method, started to study oriental styles in earnest. When worked out as an individual creation, inspired by exotically coloured music of the modern composers like Bela Bartòk and Florent Schmitt, the effect may be æsthetically satisfying, as long as there is no irritating pretence of authenticity. A Chinese princess, as danced by Doris Niles, or an oriental idol, as danced by Darja Collin, are graceful compositions in their own right, with an exotic flavour as an additional attraction. A Japanese sword dance, as interpreted by Ted Shawn, is the outcome of his training in Japanese dancing, and may therefore be considered more authentic, even if it is composed by an American. The same applies to his Red Indian dances. They always remain artistic studies of an alien race.

Of the groups of Hindu dancers who captured the pre-war world, and who later retired to their native India, those of Menaka, Uday Shankar and Ram Gopal are the best known. Nyota Inyoka, minute and supremely grace-ful, performed mainly as a solo dancer, or at best supported by a few Nautch pupils who, with the golden plumage of their widespread dance skirts, and with the musical tinkle of silver ankle-bells, accentuated the light and easy grace of these seductive dances.

The Hindu, Indradev, performed mainly with his pupil, Devaki, a Cam-bodian dancer. Authentic in the sacred dances, and purely stylized in the stronger dances of the Southern Indian *Kathakali* style, he scored also be-cause of the authenticity of the accompanying music. These dance melodies, *rhagas* and *rhaginis*, were performed by native flutes, native violins and the *tablas*, a set of drums which have to be most dexterously played.

Ram Gopal was introduced to the Western world by Serge Lifar, a few years before the outbreak of the war. His grave beauty and the magnificent restraint of his miming earned him an enviable reputation. In his small company were a few Indonesian and even Eurasian dancers; but though this might have weakened the effect of his group dances, he himself remained authentic in the traditional dances, which showed a great variety of regional Indian styles. He is a master of the static dance of the *Bharata Natya* style of South India, needing nothing more than a few square feet of ground to enact an entire story. Ram Gopal, who has studied the exacting classic Indian dance since the age of four, has now established his own school in India.

Menaka, the Hindu, and Deva Dassi, the Indonesian, were the only outstanding women dancers, as in the East the strict tradition favours female dancers only in a limited repertoire of either temple or peasant dances. Recently, however, the disturbingly beautiful Hima Kesarcodi, is gaining world recognition as a female Hindu soloist.

Much greater fame was won by the most individual of them all, the Hindu dancer, Uday Shankar, and his group. This dancer toured the Western world for some ten years before retiring to his property near Benares, where he spent the war years perfecting his art, and particularly deepening it spiritually. Here he made one of the first, and best, Indian dance films 'Kalpana'. His leaning towards mysticism was apparent from the beginning in his group dances, performed with purely Hindu artists, except for his first wife Simkie, a French girl who became, by sheer spiritual transformation, more Oriental than the Hindus themselves.

As the source of inspiration for his dance scenes, Shankar took religious subjects, and also, in a lighter vein, folk-lore of the mountaineers of the Indian borders. His hypnotic personality could electrify an enormous audience into something uncomfortably approaching hysteria. His snake-charmer's dance was uncanny in its suggestive power, but the fact that he never exploited this easy medium of personal appeal shows his artistic integrity.

To watch these legends of god and handmaiden, Indra playing with the *ghopis* (shepherdesses), Vishnu the destroyer in his wrath, and Shiva in his splendour, is like witnessing an Olympian pageant. The finger gestures of the *mudras* are like the graceful unfolding of the petals of the sacred lotus.

The true art of Asia has not been touched by Western influences, with the exception of the native musical comedy, in which jazz girls of dusky hue perform. They are sophisticated in the lavish revues of Tokyo, where the Japanese ballet-masters show the combined influence of Broadway and of Germany. But these same jazz girls are rather incongruous when they join the modest travelling shows of the Javanese dance-girls *(ronggeng)*.

The traditional ballet performances, given at the Courts of Cambodia, and of Java, are quite untouched. In Java there are two Sultans, of Souracarta (also called Solo) and of Djocjacarta, who keep their own ballet troupes. The themes of both these ballet schools are the same, but they are performed in a slightly different way. In Djocjacarta no new compositions are encouraged, and each deviation from the traditional style is censured.

In Solo, however, the ballet is more modern, which means that the strict stylization of movements remains, but that greater freedom of personal interpretation is allowed. The Hindu epic of the *Rhamajana*, ten centuries old, and the historical legends of the foundation of the Empire of Modjopahit, which disappeared in the seventeenth century, furnish the 'plots' for these ballets. A full *gamelang* orchestra, including gongs and native xylophones as well as drums, accompanies the dancing. In the Javanese theatre, the *Wayang Wong*, the plays of mostly historical origin, are also accompanied by dancing, and indeed the art of the Indonesian actor is as much that of a dancer, as is that of his Chinese and Japanese counterparts.

In Japan the most authentic traditional dancing is also seen in the theatre, in the historical *Nôh* plays. Modern solo dancers have been greatly influenced by some German teachers, who have established themselves in the capital, and by performances of travelling celebrities like Alexander Sakharoff and his wife, Clotilde von Derp, the aristocrats of the expressionist school.

Several of the outstanding solo dancers went themselves to Germany, in the first place Yoskio Aoyama, former ballet-master of a Japanese folk-ballet. He created quite a stir with his recitals in Berlin and Paris. His was the academic and traditional *Nôh* interpretation of the red-haired ape, representing the spirit of evil with a frightening mask. His was the more languid grace and harmonious fluidity of movement in the geisha dances which, according to tradition, were dance parts which could be performed on the stage by the skilled male dancers as well as by the female, and had little connection with the more monotonous ones of the real geishas of the tea-houses. His was the terrific strength of the sword dancer, with its grotesque distortions of the body, similar to those of the German school and probably, in his very personal and less authentic interpretation, influenced by it. His were, finally, the purely interpretative dances of a musical theme, often a modern Japanese composition of the composer, Yamada. These dances were neither German nor Japanese, but with an arresting mixture of both styles, which, as we have heard, he recently reproduced successfully in his mass ballets in the Imperial Opera of Tokyo.

Another Japanese dancer, Toshi Komori, who for years remained in France, mixed his styles considerably, borrowing from Korean and Polynesian folkdances. His 'soft' dances remained rather dual and vague, but in his warrior and athletic dances he was at his best. Here again it was difficult to gauge what remained authentic in his dances, and what was due to the influence of the free-movement school.

Other exotic dancers who appeared occasionally on European stages, but without reaching the general public, were of questionable authenticity; for instance, the Red Indian dancer, Oskomon, who, with his rather stolid partner, Little Elk, gave exhibitions of limited artistic interest, and even without much appeal for the anthropologist, because of the freely individual interpretation.

Since the war a new type of theatrical dance drama has come to the fore, which has probably borrowed as much of our Western ballet as of the primitive art of Darkest Africa.

Berto Pasuko was the first to bring his Negro Ballet to Europe, and to show how a theatrical instinct, schooled in the theatres of Europe, can subdue and indeed intensify the original dark rhythms of those descendants of the African negroes, who were educated in the New World.

His first electrifying success in Paris, which put him theatrically speaking on the map, may have been partly due to the surprise of a novel form of negro ballet, in which the haunting rhythms of the drums added to the terrific tension of the dancers. Born actors, like so many negroes, they gave the impression—night after night—of improvising, of being possessed, of dancing almost in a state of trance.

Among the various items, there would be several in a lighter vein, market flirtations and Carnaval dances, sometimes dangerously near the easy mark of the music-hall. But a few of the more serious dance dramas, which have remained in the repertoire, keep the stamp of authenticity and can be seen time and again without losing any of their appeal.

Such a ballet is 'The Prophet', in which the theatrically always effective miracle healing is beautifully interwoven with the hostile action of the dark, hysterical mob. Marjorie Blackman as the Priestess is one of the few strong women dancers of the company, which excels in male dancers, headed by the versatile Tommy Gomez and Pasuko himself.

The latter two rise sometimes to greatness in the barbaric tale of the coming of Christianity to the Heathens. In this, their strongest dance tale 'They came...' there is a marvellously staged battle of wills between the two groups: the medicine man with his occult power, and the soldiers of the white men.

Intricate part of the success of this cultured negro art, which yet retains so much primitive appeal, is the music. Sometimes one recognizes the piano and the familiar tunes of the negro spirituals... but mainly there are weird noises, often produced by throaty voices, which are so eminently right for this dancing. And always there is the obsession of the muffled drums, played with great virtuosity by several drummers.

After the dark, stocky, vibrant Pasuko came the glamorous, almost white American negress Dunham.

The case of Katherine Dunham, who has greatly surpassed Pasuko in public favour, is somewhat special. Her spectacles have become an intricate mixture of revue and ballet, with the spectacular side stressed more and more, and beautiful singers added to the already rich offerings of meticulously trained dancers.

With her painstaken research work, and her dance dramas, inspired on the lore of Jamaica and the West Indies, by negro rituals and spirituals, as well as by South American rhythms, she gives an almost bewildering choice of the dance idioms of the darker regions. Theatrically her presentation is superb, and her instinct almost uncanny. With her vital personality, her limited technique, and always electrifying personal sparkle she dominates each performance, in which glorious costuming and subtle lighting are as important as individual performances of each member of the cast. Lenwood Morris, her balletmaster, should come in for his share of the praise.

Although the word 'ballet' is confusing, and in fact a misnomer when talking about the Dunham group, this does not detract from its great importance as a dance spectacle, entirely unique of its kind because of its perfection of detail.

Here is the description of one of the strongest ballets from her revue 'Carribean Rhapsody':

The scene is laid in the ghostly night jungle. The ballet is called 'Shango', as the dancers, who are going to bring their offering to their God of Thunder, called Shango, execute the ceremonial dances of the West African Yoruba tribe. These dances, and the hallucinating rhythms of the drums, which accompany them, are as strong as those dances of obsession in Stravinsky's '*Sacre du Printemps*'.

The priest tends a white rooster. The Chosen One will cut its head... but the Gods do not accept his offer and the Serpent God Dambala takes possession of the body of the youth. The subsequent crowd scene, with the possessed victim in the centre, is unforgettable. The spoken word is cleverly used to augment the tension. In a final apotheosis, which again is a triumph of theatrical art showing Dunham's choreographic genius, the youth mounts a gigantic drum and is born high on this drum, which he beats frantically, hysterically...

When the curtain is lowered on this final scene of mass hysteria it seems that there can be no other climax... but when the curtain rises just once more to show the crowd, dominated by the figure on the gigantic drum, now motionless and spent, an unconscious body from which the possessed soul has departed... the impact of these primitive truths becomes greater still.

To realise such a truth in the theatre night after night one needs the purity of this negro mentality... This is, possibly, the reason why the Dunham style has made such a profound impression on the Western world, more, far more than other alien dance arts. Her dancers can teach ours sincerity and singleness of purpose... and she herself, charming as a dancer, great as a choreographer, quite simply possesses the instinct of the theatre to the nth degree. If she had chosen the opera or the straight drama as her medium, she would probably have succeeded just as spectacularly.

CHAPTER EIGHT

FAMOUS BALLET DANCERS

A king may be judged by the standard of dancing during his reign
Chinese Saying

THE ROLE OF THE DANCER

IN a work of this volume it would be impossible to present all the figures of the dance whose names have gone down in history, and all the deserving individuals of to-day. The ballets and artists mentioned, therefore, do not form a comprehensive list, but have been chosen as examples, every endeavour having been made to ensure that they are representative of the main currents of development. It must be remembered that as ballet is so much a matter of subjective reactions, any selection must, to a certain extent, be governed by personal taste.

We will first salute those great dancers of the past who have left their imprint on the history of ballet. The study of multitudes of arresting and brilliant individualities has been undertaken very thoroughly by Cyril Beaumont, and the results have been published in several of his works. Within the limited scope of this survey, an attempt has been made to outline only some figures of the best-known dancers throughout the centuries, as it seems essential that even the casual reader should at least know the greatest names.

There is a marked barrier between the solo dancers of the past and the front rankers we know to-day, who give individual recitals of their own, away from the ballet groups, in which they show other facets of their skill and talent. Those of the past, on the contrary, did not give solo recitals, but during several phases of ballet development they were allowed to dominate the group performance by their brilliance and virtuosity to such an extent that solo numbers would be arranged specially to suit their own particular skill, to be sandwiched in between the normal scenes of the ballet. This twisting of its natural flow was inclined to mar the performance as an artistic whole, the sole purpose being to allow the favourites to reap many personal laurels.

The Royal Dance Academy in Paris, originally consisting of thirteen members forming the all-powerful dance committee, was apparently unable to remedy this state of affairs, particularly as Court intrigues played a considerable part in the distribution of the leading roles. Noverre's strong hand was needed to reform the entire atmosphere and spirit of the ballet, but they deteriorated again later.

THE EIGHTEENTH CENTURY

Marie Sallé (1707–1756) was the first dancer who was bold enough to break the bonds of tradition by stressing the mimic element in her interpretation, and who generally showed a more individual and intellectual approach to the dance. Together with her rival, La Belle Camargo (1710–1770), she has gone down in history as one of the earliest dancers who really deserved the title of *prima ballerina assoluta*. She owed little to the customary Court influence and amorous intrigue, which usually ensured such a coveted position to a physically beautiful dancer.

Marie Camargo has to her credit the invention of many new steps which enriched the ballet idiom of her time, and she was the first ballerina who dared shorten the long ballet skirts in order to gain greater freedom of movement. She had a reputation for quickness combined with grace, which gave the desirable impression of effortless execution, though in fact it was based on a strict technique.

Madeleine Guimard (1743–1816) had quite a different personality. Through her life-long friendship with the notorious Prince de Soubise, whose influence reached far across the borders of France, she is reputed to have maintained her enviable position of *danseuse étoile*. However, she could not have earned a great reputation in her guest performances all over Europe if she had not also possessed an artistic quality which gave depth and strength to her technically faultless dancing.

In this Golden Age of the arts the celebrated Vestris family reigned supreme for more than a century. Gaetan Vestris, also called Vestris I (1729–1808), was the son of a dancer and an actress. He influenced ballet history in France as a dancer, choreographer and teacher. He was the perfect example of the purely classical *danseur noble*, but, lacking the facility of dance notations, his system of teaching has not been saved for posterity, as has that of his friend and colleague, Noverre. His influence on the development of ballet during his life-time was great, and for many years he enjoyed the favour of his public as first dancer. He is said to have added illiteracy and a colossal vanity to a real genius for the dance.

His son, Auguste, designated as Vestris II (1760–1842), won equal fame as a dancer, but less as ballet-master and choreographer. Father and son belonged to a century in which the *premier danseur* could hold his own with any ballerina, and was probably the greater favourite of the two. It took the subsequent romantic epoch to idealise the *danseuses*, lovely, ethereal and mysteriously remote creatures in white and diaphanous ballet-skirts, and to relegate their male partners to second or third place. The man was then reduced to mere *porteur*, lifting the ballerina, or at best to *terre à terre* character dancer. Auguste's son, therefore, following in the footsteps of his father, had less opportunity to shine, and his name is forgotten.

THE NINETEENTH CENTURY

The first half of the nineteenth century witnessed the triumph of romantic ballet, and the birth of a galaxy of stars, all women, which was typical of the epoch.

Two rivals, Sallé and Camargo, had dominated the former century, and now again two ballerinas, Marie Taglioni and Fanny Elssler, competed for first place.

Marie Taglioni was perhaps the greater of the two. She was the daughter of Filippo Taglioni, an Italian dancing master, who, at the beginning of the nineteenth century, was attached to the Paris Opera as ballet-master and choreographer. His daughter, Marie, his son, Paul, and his daughter-in-law, whose name was also Marie Taglioni, were trained by him. At the age of fifteen, in 1820, the great Taglioni made her debut at the Paris Opera, and took the world by surprise. She has been described as the most perfect vision of frail beauty ever seen on the stage, and she combined great dramatic power with unusual brilliance of technique. It was she who invented the dance *sur les pointes*, and the use of it gave to her movements the illusion of floating elevation and etherealization, which was not merely intended to dazzle the spectators, but which she considered an artistic necessity, both for the expression of a mood and for the creation of atmosphere.

Elssler was the first great dancer to appear in New York, where she presented European choreographies, particularly Auber's *La Bayadère* and one of the few ballets of the time which has survived to this day, *La Fille mal gardée*, revived recently by Ballet Theatre under the name of *Naughty Lisette*. She also danced *La Sylphide*, as much a quintessence of romantic ballet as *Giselle*, which was created by one of Taglioni's successors, Carlotta Grisi. The full points were immediately adapted by the lovely and famous Elssler. This temperamental and Spanish-looking Viennese *danseuse* was probably the greatest character dancer of her time. She was as brilliant as Taglioni, but where the one glowed the other glittered. Her Iberian *cachucha*, danced with the castanets and on the points, after the romantic style of the Spanisch ballet of that time, was acclaimed all over Europe and in America, where her triumphs made theatrical history. Another success in the style of a tempestuous folk-dance was *La Cracovienne*. Her bravura and voluptuousness made her a dazzling personality. She lived to a ripe old age in comfortable circumstances and died, a respected *bourgeoise*, in Vienna in the same year that Pavlova was born, and at a time when her former rival, in very poor circumstances, had worked herself to death as a little-appreciated ballet teacher in London (in 1884).

Other famous dancers came to the fore. Carlotta Grisi, the blonde and curved Italian, looked as agreeably and sentimentally German as the Austrian Fanny Elssler had looked Spanish. Carlotta Grisi created the title role in *Giselle* in 1841. The ballet was inspired by Théophile Gautier, who, however, passed on the writing of the libretto to a minor author, Vernoy de Saint Georges. Adam was the composer of the score and Jules Perrot, husband of Grisi, and *premier danseur* in his own right, was one of the two choreographers. It is interesting to note that the role of Albrecht was created by Lucien Petipa, brother of the famous ballet-master, Marius Petipa.

Other famous dancers of the epoch were the Italian, Fanny Cerito, and the Danish Lucille Grahn. The second part of the century witnessed an apathy in all arts and the decline of ballet. Another Danish ballerina, Adeline Genée, was the only outstanding figure at the turn of the century. She is particularly remembered for a ballet called *La Danse*, which attempted to be a sort of historical pageant of the dance between the years 1710 and 1845, and which included the works of Rameau, Lully, Corelli and Chopin.

With the appearance of Isadora Duncan and the Russian dancers another century and another epoch of dancing began.

53. Charlotta Grisi as 'Giselle', in the ballet created by her in 1841

54. Auguste Vestris (1760-1842), son of 'The divine Vestris';
balletmaster at the Paris Opera

ΤΩΝ ΜΕΝΤΟΙ ΧΗΝΩΝ ΟΥΚ
ΕΣΤΙΝ ΟΣΤΙΣ ΟΥ

55. Auguste Vestris II, his father's successor at the Opera

56. Marie Taglioni, 'La Reine de la Danse', in 1832

AND UP TO OUR OWN DAY

Two great dancers of a former generation remain in the memory as unsurpassed artists. Anna Pavlova, the 'immortal one', died at the Hague in
1931, during a farewell tour. Nijinsky died insane in 1951.

Vaslav Nijinsky, the Polish dancer, presented by Diaghilev, delighted and
surprised his Western European audiences at his debut in Paris in 1909 with
the Ballets Russes. His phenomenal leaps in *Le Spectre de la Rose* and
Scheherazade had something uncanny about them. His superb elevation and
line were the sensation of the epoch. The poet, Jean Cocteau, wrote of him:
'Il était sans cesse peint sur le plafond' —'It seemed as if he were constantly
painted on the ceiling'. It is the profound belief of those who saw him
literally float through the air, and who knew him well, that his will-power
actually retarded his descent. Like a perfect artist, he lived only for his work
until madness tragically overtook him. The book written about him by his
Rumanian wife, Romola Nijinska, gives a biased but vivid account of his
life.

Anna Pavlova was the ideal ballerina of the purely classical style. At the
Marinsky School in St. Petersburg and later at the Imperial Opera she
shared honours with Thamar Karsavina, whom she, however, soon out-
distanced in world fame. Her younger colleague, Olga Spessivtszeva, and in
our day Alicia Markova, are the only ones who resembled her in style.
From the very first, when Diaghilev introduced her to Paris, her desire to
become independent, warranted by her personal success, was apparent. With
the help of her impresario, Victor D'André, who later became her husband,
she soon formed her own company. As early as 1910 Pavlova danced *Giselle*
with her partner, Michel Mordkin, at the Metropolitan Opera in New York.
During the next ten years she was partnered successfully by Alexander
Volinine. His many successors were never quite worthy of the great
ballerina.

She created a legend of loveliness and left behind her nostalgic memories
of the romantic ballet in which she was unsurpassed. Her *Giselle* was as
dramatically moving as any ever presented, but she was also a character
dancer of passion, as she proved with her ballet, *Bacchanale*, and her dance,
Californian Poppy. She was identified, of course, with her interpretation of
Saint Saën's *Dying Swan*, one of the earliest choreographies of Fokine.

Though it has been said of Pavlova that she made her public Pavlova-conscious rather than ballet-conscious, and though undoubtedly the artistic standard of her company was not always equal to the task of supporting her in a worthy way, she contributed enormously to the popularity of ballet with her incessant tours through many remote countries. She pioneered ballet in such places as South America, the Indies, and Australia.

The general standard of the present-day companies is as high, perhaps, as ever it was, and though the star system is not so much favoured, there are, all the same, some very outstanding soloists in every company. Consequently many artists creating roles to-day would be worthy of record, though only the lapse of time would lend a true perspective to their comparative merits. Dancers of either sex win equal fame, though at present the scales swing more towards the male dancers, because many of them are important choreographers as well, interpreting their own work.

Of such choreographers we merely recall Leonid Massine, Balanchine, Serge Lifar, David Lichine, Roland Petit, Frederick Ashton, Antony Tudor, and Kurt Jooss in another field. The last three are less conspicuous as dancers. The important female choreographers of to-day are Bronislava Nijinska, Ninette de Valois, Andrée Howard, and certainly Agnes de Mille and Janine Charrat.

Of the outstanding dancers of our own era we mention Serge Lifar, André Eglevsky, Youskevitch, Jean Babilée, and of the ballerinas Alexandra Danilova, Alicia Markova, Galina Ulanova, Tatiana Riabouchinska, Irina Baronova, Tamara Toumanova, Margot Fonteyn, Rosella Hightower, Yvette Chauviré, Nora Kaye, and Maria Tallchief.

Of the outstanding male dancers, British Anton Dolin, and the Australian Robert Helpmann were perhaps the most versatile, being both good dancers and good mimes. If Helpmann is the only one whose career is discussed here in detail, it is not because he should be considered as the best dancer-choreographer of our time, but because the limited scope of this book does not allow a similar study of them all.

In the next chapter a few of the outstanding choreographers are reviewed, but Helpmann somehow seems not quite to fit in, because his merits as a dancer and interpreter of his own work form an integral part of his own ballets, whereas as an interpreter of classic and modern repertoires he is definitely a great dancer in his own right.

Helpmann's career is the more interesting because his youth was misspent, from a ballet point of view. Unlike most of the great classic dancers, who start training at the age of ten, Helpmann had passed adolescense when he took his first serious ballet lessons with Laurent Novikov, then touring Australia as Pavlova's partner.

He went to London, and in 1933 he was dancing in the *corps de ballet* of the newly formed Sadler's Wells company, benefiting from the lessons of Ninette de Valois, who is reported to have said, when the young Australian presented himself: 'I can do something with that face'.

His early association with Vivien Leigh and Sir Laurence Olivier may have helped to develop his histrionic ability. The fact is that his first success in the Sadler's Wells company was established in a part in which miming and a perfect sense of timing were as important as the dancing. This was in de Valois' *The Rake's Progress*. In the meantime, alternating with Dolin, he had partnered Markova and the budding ballerina, Margot Fonteyn, in purely classic ballets, such as *Les Sylphides* and *Aurora's Wedding*.

At the outbreak of the war he had become the undisputed first dancer of the company, and the ideal partner for the maturing talent of Margot Fonteyn. His creation, in 1940, of the part of Mr. O'Reilly in *The Prospect Before Us* established him as the foremost comedy dancer of London.

Under the most difficult circumstances and the terrific strain of the war years he established his reputation as a choreographer whose works, in a sense, have modified the structure of the ballet in England. He added to his fame the reputation of being a Shakespearian actor of authority, and a screen actor as well, even though in this last capacity he was indifferently successful.

His first ballet of importance, which probably will survive our days, was *Comus*. Helpmann composed this work, as inspired by Milton's poem, to Purcell's music. He incorporated in his production the beautiful verse of Milton, impeccably spoken as well as danced by himself.

His sensational *Hamlet* followed, with the potent and lurid *décor* of Leslie Hurry, placing this artist at one stroke in the front rank of ballet designers. Hurry followed this up with an equally astonishing new *décor* for *Swan Lake*.

Helpmann scored a double success by acting the part of Hamlet opposite Pamela Brown and in the same year dancing the part with Margot Fonteyn. This was a feat without precedent in the ballet world.

Other creations, such as *Adam Zero* and *Miracle in the Gorbals*, followed, always in the first place vehicles for his own particular talents. *Adam Zero* is reported to be brilliant, cynical and detached, the story of Adam translated in terms of a ballet in the making. The three Fates are in the guise of the Designer, the Wardrobe Mistress, and the Dresser. With different wigs placed upon his head, Adam ages before our eyes. His lifeline is shortened, then snapped, as the ballet proceeds.

Though his critics have objected that his ballets contain everything but dancing, and though he himself, as a magnificent mime, undoubtedly dominates each production with his personality, it must be said that all he does is supremely dramatic. He has that sixth sense of the artist which can discriminate instinctively between good and bad stagecraft. His style of choreography shows a happy tendency to incorporate deeper dramatic feeling and freer movement in the framework of the ballet, which remains strictly based on classic technique.

CHAPTER NINE

CHOREOGRAPHY AND CHOREOGRAPHERS

He who realises the Power of the Dance rests in God
Hindu Proverb

BACKGROUND

WHEN considering the individual qualities of an artist it is often difficult to ascertain where the dancer ends and the choreographer begins. This is particularly the case when considering such ballets as those of Helpmann, Lifar, and Lichine, who dance the principal parts of their own creations.

The quality of the dancer's interpretation is not only determined by the technical and histrionic rendering of his part, but also by the ingenuity of the choreographer in combining solo dancing and group dancing. The dancer furthermore contributes his own temperament and physical suitability to the part.

In unconnected solo dances, customary at dance recitals, the interpreter is often his or her own choreographer. One of the most famous classical solo dances, probably more often performed than any other separate dance of a *divertissement*, is *The Dying Swan*, which was arranged by Fokine for Pavlova. Excerpts of classic ballets, either *pas seul* or *pas de deux*, are naturally performed in the authentic form laid down by the choreographer. But in the freer interpretations of the modern-academic as well as of the expressionist dances most performers arrange their own numbers.

The creative work thus involved is obviously far easier than when creating an entire ballet, where whole groups and important musical scores are being handled.

As dancing is entirely an art of visual expression, an indifferent suite of music can be superbly danced and thus saved from mediocrity by the talent of the performer. Vice versa it is obvious that a splendid musical score can be spoiled entirely by poor choreography or by indifferent performers. From this one may assume that character dancers—mime and *terre-à-terre* dancers —have more chance of bringing individual improvisations to their parts, because such parts may vary more in mood and colour than those of the classic dancer, whose every movement is strictly controlled. But nevertheless the actual personality and temperament of the classical dancer is of the greatest importance. It is always essential to a completely satisfying performance that one should be aware of that mysterious interflow of inner rhythm, balance and precision of movement on the part of the dancer. And that quality, just as much as purity of line, is a gift of the gods, which can be developed by training, but never acquired by schooling alone.

The evolution of the modern academic ballet shows the primary importance of the choreographer's function, which reflects the spirit of our day, with its heart-throb and laughter, its intellectual approach and its conception of beauty.

Before 1900 a complete merger of the theatrical arts in ballet was seldom attempted. In a few isolated cases it succeeded supremely well, as, for instance, when the ballet, *Giselle*, was created by the simultaneous efforts of all the artists concerned. It survived, because real works of art are not concerned with passing fashions, but possess the imperishable appeal of beauty.

It was not until the Diaghilev era that a perfect blending was achieved of music, choreography, dancing and line and colour. The last comprised *décor*, costume, make-up and lighting, buth with a much more sober use of props and mechanical tricks than had been the vogue during the preceding period of decline.

During the three centuries of our ballet history there have been several peaks of dramatic intensity of interpretation, alternating with other periods of a mere display of virtuosity. At the turn of this century ballet was in the rigid bonds of convention. It had started with the heroic and allegoric subjects favoured in the early days, giving way to romantic themes, which in their turn had passed into limbo in the eighties, to be replaced by tricks and triteness. Costumes throughout had been dictated by convention. When, in the days of Petipa at the Marinsky Theatre, or at the Paris Opera, a Greek style was required, the ballerina kept to her regulation *tutu* and simply added a slight touch of tunic, or breastplates, or ribbons to her bodice, in order to give local colour. It needed a strong personality to get rid of these inhibitions and break the bonds of æsthetic slavery. This strong personality was Michel Fokine.

THE MASTER CHOREOGRAPHER

The aims of contemporary choreography have been laid down by Fokine, in his credo, published in *The Times* on the 6th July, 1914, which we reproduce as summarized by Arnold Haskell:

> To invent in each case a new form of movement, corresponding to the subject and character of the music, instead of merely giving combinations of ready-made steps.
>
> Dancing and gesture have no meaning in ballet, unless they serve as an expression of dramatic action.
>
> To admit the use of conventional gesture only when it is required by the style of the ballet, and in all other cases to replace the gestures of the hands by movements of the whole body. Man can, and should be, expressive from head to foot.
>
> The group is not merely an ornament. The new ballet advances from the expressiveness of the face or the hands to the whole body, and from that of the individual body to groups of bodies, and the expressiveness of the combined dancing of a crowd.
>
> The alliance of dancing on equal terms with the other arts.
>
> The new ballet does not demand "ballet music" from the composer, nor *tutus* and pink satin slippers from the artist; it gives complete liberty to their own creative powers.

Fokine's last statement should be amended. He advocates complete liberty, but he overrides the urge of the dancer to contribute a personal note, moulding him to his vision. Because of this he achieved unity and smoothness from beginning to end. The executive artist contributes little to the whole but his dancing ability.

Many ballets of the pre-Fokine period do not stand up to scrutiny and, when analysed, are reduced to a series of dances interpolated in the mimed action, mere excuses for the exhibition of virtuosity. The miming, merely outlined by the choreographer, left the dancer very much to his own devices.

Fokine made mimed action and dancing one. The dancing became expressive in itself, and less traditional.

But where then, one may ask, lies the difference between this conception of the dance and the aim of a Rudolph von Laban or a Mary Wigman? They also wanted to be expressive in the first place.

This may be true, but they over-emphasized their wish. They invented their peculiar form of expressionist dancing because they wanted to externalize their emotions at any cost—and that cost included the sacrifice of technique and of style, and of the meaning of the music.

Fokine, on the other hand, conceived expressiveness in terms of ballet deportment, and this new freedom of ballet continued to acknowledge its tradition of style and technique. He accepted the geometry underlying classical ballet structure, and in so doing he kept to a logically built-up movement.

The geometrical basis of a ballet does not, as one might think, limit and formalize its emotional interpretation. On the contrary it enriches expression as we become aware of the existence of this design. The interest grows as we discern more clearly the variety of lines, the contrast of opposing groups, and the position of the soloist against the background of the *corps de ballet*. The contrast of lines might be compared with that between rhythm and counter-rhythm. Thus the force of expression is enhanced.

Of all the Fokine ballets *Petrouchka*, with its Russian folk-lore, its deep underlying meaning and its moving 'tear-stained brightness', gave perhaps the greatest impetus to later intellectual ballets. Composed in the best Diaghilev vein, it was the joint product of Fokine, Benois and Stravinsky. If *Giselle* remains one of the most complex and beautiful roles for a classic dancer, the doll in *Petrouchka* is a worthy counterpart, as it combines the mechanical and the human with extreme delicacy.

There are several explanations of the real meaning of this dance story. One of them is that the dancing of the Doll, the Blackamoor, and Petrouchka portrays the eternal clash between true and false love, and the feminine incapacity for understanding either! Other interpretations are, of course, possible. Several authors, intrigued by the alleged 'secret meaning' of it all, were pleased to discover a sublimated melancholia *(Weltschmerz)* in it. This interpretation may be also true. And again, it may be a portrayal of human impotence battling with Fate. It does not really matter. Petrouchka cannot fail to move us. And therein lies its greatness.

A life-time of great choreographies lies between Fokine's first works in the grand manner, such as *Scheherazade* and *Cléopâtre*, and his last ballet, *Bluebeard*, created in 1941 to music by Jacques Offenbach. It has been said that the theme is fantastically complicated, but that the choreography, with its witty comedy parts, abounds in finds of character dancing. It proved that Fokine's death interrupted a creative career, which might have yielded many more masterpieces. After his death America's Ballet Theatre showed the ballet he had been preparing, Prokofiev's '*The Russian soldier*'.

LEONID MASSINE

A great deal has been said in the past, and will be said in the future, about Massine (pronounced Miassin). To follow his development from his early

57.   George Balanchine, the great choreographer, renovator of American ballet

58. Margot Fonteyn, Robert Helpmann, and Celia Franca in 'Hamlet'

59. Les Ballets des Champs Elysées in 'The Devil's Bride' with Roland Petit

60. Building up a movement at rehearsal (Ballet des Champs Elysées)

61. Helpmann's ballet 'Adam Zero' at Covent Garden

62. Antony Tudor as Tybalt in his own production of 'Romeo and Juliet',
Ballet Theatre, New York

63. Irina Baronova and Anton Dolin rehearse

64.   Leonid Massine and Hélène Kirsova in 'Choreartium'

Diaghilev ballets to his later symphonic works is to follow the entire evolution of modern ballet. His deep knowledge of the theatre and of music, and his peculiar genius for dance designs, made all he ever did of interest. There may be uneven Massine ballets, but there are no indifferent ones. In all of them his famous architectural tableaux are a feature of each scene.

He served his own dance talent well, but most of his works have been interpreted with equal success by other dancers. His bar-tender in *Union Pacific* (one of the first ballets inspired by American pioneer history) and his hussar in *Beau Danube* are memorable. As a partner in a classic *pas de deux*, however, he is less remarkable, because of his slight build.

He made, and continues to make, an intensive study of art museums, maintaining that the ballet may be three hundred years old, but that the pictorial arts are many thousands. He has found that choreography must be based upon a sequence of movements which follow definite laws. If there is no system, it fails as an art. He has elaborated on Noverre's system and hopes that, one day, he will be able to teach it to others.

His symphonic ballets—*Les Présages*, to Tchaikovsky's Fifth, *Choreartium* to Brahm's Fourth, *Symphonie fantastique* to the Berlioz symphony, and *Rouge et Noir* to Shostakovitch's First Symphony—are milestones on the road to future developments. In these abstract choreographies one finds definite traces of the Central-European schools. Why, then, is the Massine version of this system so superior? It is the steadying hand of untroubled classical purity which one feels, and the confidence which it gives. Throughout their design these choreographic lines run parallel with the music, without any aim at trying to 'translate' the music, which would be impossible. But all the movements of the dance are intensely musical. Never was Massine's architectural structure more harmonious than in his last symphonic ballet to date, *Rouge et Noir*, created in 1939.

A penetrating study of Massine's works has been made by Adrian Stokes, in his book, *Russian Ballets*, which makes their significance quite clear.

The relation between the dancers themselves is most important; the masses are working together with, or against, the solo dancer, who breaks away, only to be swallowed again by the mass movement. It seems as if all possible variations of movement and line have been summoned by Massine to the dancer's aid. And there is, throughout, the most intimate connection between the dancing and the music.

Massine's Spanish folk-ballet, *The Three-cornered Hat*, a triumph of folk-dance adapted to ballet, has been mentioned before. Another early ballet, in a lighter vein, was *La Boutique fantasque*, produced for Diaghilev in 1919, and often revived since. This gay and artless *ballet d'action* has a variety of highly effective parts and the dancing includes a *divertissement*, which shows them all off to advantage and gives proof of Massine's absolute mastery of his medium. When more sophisticated ballets have been forgotten, *La Boutique fantasque* will still be the delight of children of all ages.

For the last few years Massine has divided his time between the ballet companies of many countries. We see him with a Flemish ballet 'Le Bal du Pont du Nord' at the Opera Comique, where he also restages an old favourite 'Caprice Espagnol'. Then he is at the Covent Garden to mount for the Sadlers Wells company a Scottish ballet 'Donald of the Burthens', which is an interesting failure, although it shows the mastery of Beryl Grey as the dominating figure of Death. Haydn's 'Clock Symphony' is a greater success, but a restaging of the 'Three-Cornered Hat' shows that a substitute for his own interpretation of the Miller's part weakens the ballet as a whole.

Massine is still full of energy and invention, which he will also use for the ever-developing possibilities of film and television. Although his last works haven't been sensational we may still expect some high-grade surprises from this quarter.

GEORGE BALANCHINE AND OTHERS

Balanchine was a pupil of the Imperial School of St. Petersburg, and stayed in Russia after the revolution to perfect his art. He was one of the few Soviet artists who joined Diaghilev, in 1925. He had absorbed the Soviet belief in art reform, as outlined in the theatre by Meyerhold and Stanislavsky, who added physical training and even acrobatic training, to the actor's education.

His first ballet, produced for Diaghilev, revealed this trend. His style, though purely academic, showed a certain lack of elevation, stressing the *terre-à-terre* qualities of the character dancers. Often it was rhythmical acrobatics more than ballet dancing.

He studied the more mature style of his colleagues, Massine and Nijinska, whom he succeeded as the last choreographer of the Diaghilev company. Aiming at the elimination of his Russian style, he produced the still acrobatic *Apollon Musagètes* to a score of Stravinsky, and *The Prodigal Son* of Prokofiev, which brought the two exiled Soviet artists together.

During subsequent years Balanchine was mainly active in the United States, where his style underwent many modifications. Important works were created for his American Ballet, the Ballet Russe, and Ballet Theatre. He passed through many stages and, curiously enough, some of his best works were conceived as vehicles for particular dancers. His witty ballet, *La Concurrence*, exploited the brilliance of Tamara Toumanova, in 1932 still a 'baby-ballerina'. Two years later he produced *Serenade*, which for the first time gave an inkling of his neo-classic approach to choreographic problems.

In one of the recent Stravinsky ballets, *Danses Concertantes*, there is a strong flavour of the *commedia dell'arte*, exploiting the sparkling personality of Alexandra Danilova. Balanchine has been Artistic Director of the world-famous New York City Ballet since 1948. This company, which dances primarily a galaxy of Balanchine's modern classical masterpieces, has been acclaimed not only in America, but throughout Europe, where it has recently toured. Balanchine's contribution to musical comedy dancing, together with the new classical style he has developed, make him indeed the renovator of American ballet.

In any further survey of choreographers Bronislava Nijinska should have first honours, because of the important works she created, and because of the influence many of her daring experiments had on others.

In France, Serge Lifar and Roland Petit, with his *Ballets des Champs Elysées*, are equally famous. Janine Charrat, who wanders in and out of the Opera and the other French ballet troupes, displaying both her creative talent as a choreographer and her fine qualities as a dancer, is an ornament of French ballet.

Ninette de Valois, Helpmann, Ashton, Howard and Walter Gore must be considered the pillars of British ballet; whereas the British Antony Tudor triumphs in America, and Skibine with the Cuevas Ballet all over the world.

All these, and other choreographers, are in full production, and are evolving gradually a style of their own, the value of which is evident, but cannot as yet be assessed exactly. The future will show who among them will be the leaders, and with so many talent to choose from the future can take care of itself.

CHAPTER TEN

ELEMENTS OF THE STAGE DANCE

Dancing means Music made visible
Theophile Gautier
All dances, even comical ones, have dramatic possibilities
Leonid Massine

MUSIC

USIC is almost always the motive force of the dance and, where interpretative dancing is concerned, it should be the main source of the dancer's inspiration. Dancing is almost never self-sufficient. Rhythmic bodily movements may express the emotions, but for the regulation of the gestures and attitudes of the dancers a form of accompaniment is required. Whether it be simple hand-clapping or a symphonic orchestra is immaterial, as both serve the same purpose.

When the theatrical dancer wants to express emotions he must observe all the elements of musical phrasing, shading, time and dynamics present in the accompaniment. Melodic lines and rhythmic patterns must be followed closely. The play of the limbs is actuated by the melodic movement, pauses being translated by attitudes. The truly creative dancer must, therefore, possess musical sense and must study the two arts supporting stage dance and ballet: painting and music.

Gesture by itself counts for very little. Its value depends on the emotion inspiring it. The music of sound controls and refines the music of movement. When there is no complete unity of their two rhythms the artistic integrity of the presentation is impaired, unless, of course, contrast of rhythm should be consciously used to strengthen the interpretation. Jacques Dalcroze, the father of eurhythmics, expressed this thought very clearly: 'Each musical composition comprises an element of inspiration, of thematic development, and of structure. It may be expressed in various ways by various dancers, according to their temperament and technique'.

A Duncan in immobility, a Sakharoff in diversity of gesture, or a Pavlova in movement can be all equally right in their interpretation of the same piece of music. So long as they are inspired by the 'soul' of the music (as we must call it for want of a better word), their various interpretations can be equally moving, although they all use their own particular medium.

In the growth of ballet it has been observed that, at its best, it is the sum total of many individual efforts. A ballet such as *Choreartium* shows that a symphony can be plastically interpreted in pure line and mood, standing by itself as a dance creation running parallel with the music. There is no intellectual support from a plot, or notes in the programme to explain its meaning to the audience. The atmosphere is created without specifying any particular period of history or any specific *mise-en-scène*. Nor are there any literary associations.

Music written for the accompaniment of folk-dancing has influenced music for the ballet, just as the steps of folk-dances have been incorporated in ballet technique. Little has survived from ancient times.

One five-part suite of antique Greek dances has been unearthed and, thanks to the revival of the Greek dance, it was reconstructed after 1900. It is called *Niobe*, and consists of a *Prelude*, a *Challenge*, *The Combat*, *The Resting Time*, and *Victory*.

The mediæval folk-dances of Europe, sometimes of religious significance, were followed by the more mundane Italian French suite with its *rigaudon*, *gaillarde*, *courante*, *passacaille*, *allemande*, *minuet* and *gavotte*. Lully, who composed several of these suites, was indeed the first composer who actually wrote specific music of quality for an entire ballet, consisting of a sequence of dances for a Court pageant.

The sonata was the logical outcome of the suite, and Scarlatti, Bach, Mozart and Beethoven composed music which was frequently inspired by current dance themes. These themes formed the material out of which later ballet music was assembled.

The nineteenth century was the era of the *polka* and the *waltz*. It was the romantic period of Strauss and Weber, of Chopin and of Liszt. The *polonaise* was the choreographic glorification of the Polish man, and the *mazurka* was danced as its feminine counterpart. The *gopak* of Russia, the *czardas* of Hungary, the *tarantella* of Italy and the various *jotas* and *seguidillas* of Spain furnished further dance material, as well as musical themes, for the ballet.

Our own century has contributed the *cake-walk*, which was the first negro dance to be seen in polite society. Then came the *tango* and the *jazz*, with its syncopation. The *blues* and the Mexican *rumba* came next, and recently even such dances as the *big apple* have found their way into American ballet (*Union Pacific*, *Rodeo*, *Billy the Kid*, and *Fancy Free.*)

DANCE STYLE

The main inspiration of dancing is not always music. It may be pure rhythm. In most primitive tribal dances the rhythm is marked by hand-clapping, stamping of the feet and the use of percussion instruments. In the less primitive, but certainly as unsophisticated folk-dances of the gipsies and the Spaniards, it is the same. Sometimes there is a song to explain the meaning underlying the action of the dance.

The dance may then become a social function, or a martial or religious ceremony, from which would be naturally excluded any attempt at interpreting the music, which is the aim of stage dancing.

It is quite possible to dance without the accompaniment of music, on the stage or anywhere else. We have witnessed the attempts of the expressionist schools of Central Europe to express pure movement artistically, and unaided by any musical accompaniment. Outside the studio they were rarely a success, though they may have been of interest as experiments. They made one aware of the limited range of effective gestures and attitudes which, without the aid of the music, are never strong enough to carry conviction.

Music may suggest a definite style of dance, or a specific epoch. The orchestral colour of a score of Bach suggests lofty mediæval cloisters and churches. The Polovtsian dances from *Prince Igor* are the visual and logical outcome of Borodin's barbaric richness and vigour of melody. The brooding intentness of Stravinsky's score for *Le Sacre du Printemps* set the key for the mood of the whole dance production, later interpreted in a different but happy vein by Walt Disney in his film, *Fantasia*.

When a choreographer pictures the music of *Cimarosiana* in scenes of early Italian atmosphere, which are historically correct for this music, then *décor* and dancing will have to accentuate this style, in order to achieve unity. If the music is of a romantic period then it may be expected that the stage vision will be romantic, with the dancers attired in the traditional tights and ballet skirts.

This refers to the choreographies which are built round existing music. Often, however, the composer is commissioned to write ballet-music in collaboration with the choreographer, who has a definite idea of what he wants to achieve. In this case a sequence of dances has sometimes already been worked out in detail before the composition of the music which may have a definite value of its own, but again may be indifferent programme music. The piano suite composed for the best work of Kurt Jooss, *The Green Table*, is an example of the latter.

A great composer such as Tchaikovsky can, on the other hand, infuse genuine inspiration into ballet music made to order, although working within the limits imposed by the frame-work of the choreography. In his biography, by M. Tchaikovsky, we find an amusing example of what he had to put up with. The ballet-master, Marius Petipa, when arranging the *Nutcracker Suite*, handed him the entire composition worked out on paper, thus:

1. Music for dance—64 beats.
2. The tree is lit up—sparkling music 8 beats.
3. Children's entrance—boisterous music 24 beats.
4. A moment of astonishment—tremolo of several beats.
5. March of 64 beats.

and so on, until the final curtain. The music of *Casse-Noisette*, needless to say, did not suffer from this treatment in the hands of such a master.

At one of the final rehearsals it became apparent that the music would end before the back-drop had been changed. Tchaikovsky was requested to add enough music to cover the time required for the unfolding of a few more yards of *décor*. This piece has been called the 'yard music'. Such extreme cases of laying down the law to a composer are rarely encountered.

There is, finally, another method of constructing a stage dance. It can be done without a detailed choreography. The dance, in such cases, is merely made to express the rhythmic moods evoked by the music, in a more or less abstract way. The mood may be of gaiety or of anguish, or of any of the emotions, obeying the flux of the music but, contrary to the character dance, no literary association is required.

Musical thought can be appreciated for itself alone. It does not really need a visual or a literary aid. But when the dance makes us aware of the profound connection between musical thought and plastic presentation of this thought, our perception of the work is deepened. Ballet may not, of itself, help us to understand music in the way in which music contributes to the triumph of ballet, but when the two arts join forces there is a greater chance of understanding their mutual aim more easily.

DÉCOR

The choreographer has another powerful aid with which to express his meaning. *Décor* and costume are an integral part of the whole production.

In the beginning dancing was of necessity performed in the open air. Its natural background was a meadow in the spring, a forest under the moon, or perhaps the inner court of a temple. Even in the days of Court pageantry it did not require the adjunct of much scenery. Folk-dancing had for its appropriate setting the village square or green, and the revived Hellenic dancing was more often than not performed against a background of black curtains, and did not rely on a vista of the Acropolis to give it its proper atmosphere.

The theatre, naturally, requires the optical illusion of a stage setting. For centuries, however, the back-drops and the costumes for ballet were singularly conventional and uninspired. No artist of merit would lower himself by painting meaningless columns or life-size effigies of the Muses on the canvas of the flats, which in any case served only as a frame for all sorts of different productions.

The modern conception of the dance as interpretation of musical thought has improved the visual spectacle, by adding the æsthetic satisfaction of appropriate *décor* and costumes.

The atmosphere of the scene and the entire gamut of the emotions can be pictorially expressed in the *décor* which may be altered by the magic of lighting.

Our contemporary painters collaborated enthusiastically. They understood that it was their job to give a permanent form to the artistic ideals of their era, and when dressing the ballet they contributed a real factor of visual appeal. They freed the ballet from its conventional prettiness and from the laborious pomp and ugliness of Victorian days.

Sometimes their part of the success of a ballet was greater than that of the composer and the choreographer. This was particularly the case in the third period of the Diaghilev era, the period of its decline. Masters like Picasso, Derain and Braque had more to say than the choreographers in some of the 'intellectual' ballets which were then the vogue.

There are several *décors* which remain famous in ballet history because of their influence on other contemporary arts. Léon Bakst, with the gaudy opulence and the barbaric splashes of brilliant colour in his oriental designs

65. XIXth Century Spanish Style: Fanny Elssler in her celebrated Cachucha,
created in 1836

66. William Constable's aboriginal decor for 'Terra Australis' (Borovansky Ballet)

67. Loudon Sainthill, wellknown London designer, made his first ballet decor for 'Vieux Paris' (Kirsova company, Sydney)

70.   Imaginative costumes for Stravinsky's 'Jeu des Cartes',
Ballet Champs-Elysées production

67. Loudon Sainthill, wellknown London designer, made his first ballet decor for 'Vieux Paris' (Kirsova company, Sydney)

68. Serge Lifar in the Fokine version of 'Daphnis and Cloé' at the Paris Opera

69.   English version of Ravel's 'Daphnis and Chloé' at the Sadler's Wells, with prima
ballerina Margot Fonteyn and Alexander Grant

70. Imaginative costumes for Stravinsky's 'Jeu des Cartes',
Ballet Champs-Elysées production

71. With flowing scarves Janine Charrat creates the mood of Debussy's music. She is Lifar's most promising pupil-choreographer

72. Ballet Workshop, London's latest experimental ballet. David Paltenghi's 'Scherzi del Destino' with a Leslie Hurry decor

for *Scheherazade* shocked a surprised public into delirious abuse or exalted appreciation. There was the gaudy fairyland of Gontcharova's *Coq d'Or*, the gaily Russian atmosphere of Benois' *Petrouchka*, and the sober, almost abstract stylization of all things Spanish given by Picasso in the *décor* of *The Three-cornered Hat*. There was the strange play of glimmering lights in the shining mica setting which Braque invented for *The Cat*, or the bare dignity of wide spaces, created by a simple juxtaposition of primary colours, as achieved by Larionov, Derain, and Matisse.

Some of the prewar fashion dictators tried their hand at ballet costumes, without striking success. Paul Poiret, 'Coco' Chanel (during the time when she helped Diaghilev financially), Madeleine Vionnet and Maggy Rouff all dressed ballets. More recently the late Christian Bérard, Pierre Balmain and Christian Dior achieved some really beautiful costumes, particularly for the period-style classic ballet.

Really good *décor*, like a really good dance costume, should explain itself, be it realistic or stylized. It should not be too striking, nor too blotchy. It should be merely a background for groups and figures, and it should support the action and reflect the spirit of the choreographer's work. In fact it should follow the multiple and very special laws of the theatre, and make all allowances for the different approaches of reality, necessitated by the different perspective of the stage.

That is the reason why in some instances a plain back-drop may be preferable to a poorly painted one. The black curtains, used so often for a presentation of solo dancers or for expressionist dance-stories, may be adequate, particularly if insufficient lighting equipment is available. In a flat light the movements of the dancing figures are more easily discernible against such a stark background. But grey curtains give a much softer effect, as long as the individual dancers and the groups can be focused clearly in the lights of the projectors.

Some famous painters are never able to achieve satisfactory stage designs, whereas others, who may be indifferent painters, possess an instinctive theatrical sense and are able to design for the ballet. Several of the best-known designers for contemporary ballet have only been outstanding in that particular field.

Sometimes the pictorial side of the ballet has been over-emphasized, to the detriment of the production. In creating the atmosphere for a ballet it should never be allowed to detract from the dancing or mime by possessing an insidious or too obvious a presence. Leslie Hurry's admirable *Hamlet* δ*écor* might be taken as an example of this. Its faintly surrealistic designs, the clutching fists holding giant daggers dripping with blood, the winding stair-cases coiling like evil serpents, all these partake of the nightmare and suggest a state of torment, which is eminently suitable for this ballet. But its atmosphere is too overwhelming, and thereby defeats its own ends.

Simplified and over-stylised decor can be mannered and too pretentious. Salvator Dali's too self-consciously surrealistic decor (as for the Wagnerian *Mad Tristan*) were merely amusing and the corps de ballet girls, showing on one side feminine underwear, on the other man's shorts, garters and socks, might have earned their applause in revue.

The sculptural and very simple 'contructivist' decors of the Japanese-American Isamu Noguchi, mainly working for Martha Graham, are the exception to the rule. For this type of dancing they are admirably right.

Stylized δ*écor* which either merely indicates period and country, or suggests an atmosphere with single strokes of the brush and vivid play of space and colour, are almost always ideal for ballet. The value of strongly contrasted colour schemes composed of groups of dancers, detaching themselves from a violently coloured back-drop, has been never more clearly demonstrated than by Henri Matisse in the δ*écor* of Massine's symphonic ballet, *Rouge et Noir*. The tableaux were after the style of abstract paintings, with a back-cloth of primary yellows and greens, against which the groups made solid masses of moving reds and whites.

COSTUME

A good character costume should explain itself, and if it were to walk across the stage of its own volition, or merely supported by some sort of an invisible man, the audience should know at once what kind of person was supposed to wear the costume.

It should also explain the mood and the musical colour of the dance, and give the spectator, from the very moment of its entrance, a key to its atmos-phere. In a more abstract rendering, line, colour and material become the main concern.

A costume for dancing must look equally well in movement and in repose. During the most strenuous exercise it must remain intact, and it must never impede the movements of the dance. Furthermore, costumes should never be so elaborate as to detract from the quality of the dance. Ballet is not revue.

All these points should be considered when assessing the value of the costume designer's very important contribution to the dance. As the effect of line is always his primary concern, he should give great attention to hairdressing and all that goes with it. In some of the more turbulent and emotional dances, where a climax is produced by an acceleration of speed, beats and turns, the effect of a coil of hair coming undone may be intentional, and may, as a natural aid, increase the dramatic intensity—but it must never be accidental.

Consequently an invisible or decorative hair-net can be an important part of the costume, saving the dancer embarrassment, and actually adding to the value of her appearance. Other important aids are make-up, wigs, a tattoo painted on a sailor's arm, or paddings to suggest grotesque rotundities. Wigs in particular may be fantastic, and made out of unusual materials, such as tinfoil, wire, rope, silk braid, or transparant plastic.

Simplicity and economy of line and colour are the constant concern of the costume designer, who often is also responsible for the curtains and the scenery of a ballet. He must think in terms of the grouping of all the characters on the stage, of the solo dancers detaching themselves sufficiently against the background of the *corps de ballet*, and of them both against the towering mass of the back-cloth.

For this reason the costumes of the *corps de ballet* have to be conceived as an entity, in which the various flashes and contradictions of colour must never clash. In the same way the colour of the back-drop and of the framing flats must be considered, as they have to absorb the various shades of lighting, and remain effective under the varying intensity of the projectors.

Roughly speaking, the same law applies on the stage as in decorative painting. There are the cold colour ranges of blues and greens, and the warmer ones of yellow-reds to purple. Black ties them together. Dead white is almost never used—there is a stage superstition that it is an unlucky colour—but the off-whites and pink-whites can very well complete a warm-toned scheme.

Sometimes the costumes have to follow certain conventions of style. When a *bourrée* is danced, for example, its peasant origin suggests a looped skirt and a shawl. A Spanish Court dance such as the *pavane* (the paecock dance) is arrogant and stately, and calls for a period costume which hints at social prestige and affluence.

But often pure phantasy can reign supreme, and then many unusual materials can be used. Cellophane and straw, stiff gauze and metal-threaded cloth, barbaric-looking jewellery made from gilded cork, and cheap cottons sprayed with light reflecting dyes.

Accessories can enhance effects, from a fan and a flower to a single glove or a bright bow, tied above the knee and revealed only in dancing. Sleeves, girdles and square necklines can subtly suggest an Egyptian style or the period of Florentine Renaissance. Gay suspenders or incongruous pleats jutting out at the back may accentuate the comic effect of a dance. A long strip of blue gauze, trailing over a dress of silvery grey, may accentuate the mood of Debussy's *Clair de Lune*. For that matter, softly flowing scarves, which can be draped differently or trail at the back, are often used in the repertoire of expressionist dancers.

When national costume is required for the stage adaptation of peasant dances, it is often more practical to use only the essential elements and details of the folk-dress, rather than aim at absolute authenticity. Too much is always worse than too little, and their variety of colours and their gaudy embroideries, though delightful enough, would probably appear flat and dull, when seen under strong stage lighting, and from across the space of the footlights.

The various colour slides used in the projectors are powerful aids to the creation of atmosphere, and may even change the effect of the same costume. The American ballet of Loie Fuller gained international fame with its dances of light and shade, almost exclusively achieved by a most intricate and effective lighting system, and by the use of luminous costumes and phosphorescent back-drops.

CHAPTER ELEVEN

LITERATURE AND THE BALLET

With Dance begins the ballet; when Dance is absent
the ballet cannot begin
M. Gabrovich

BALLET AND DANCE THEATRE

DIFFERENT trends in literature have from time to time influenced the development of ballet. This influence, however, was only slight and incidental until the rejuvenation of ballet in the twentieth century, when the outcrop of new intellectual efforts constituted a healthy revolt against the trite ballet themes of late-Victorian days.

The high technical standard of the dancers remained, but it was not so obviously stressed. Mere exhibitions of virtuosity were driven into the background, and only required when the part called for a particular display of technical brilliance. The choreographer was no longer self-sufficient: he had to work in close collaboration with the writer of the 'book'.

This trend was even more apparent in the 'expressive ballets' of the Central European School, constituting in embryo the dance theatre which, particularly in the United States, has become a separate *native* branch of the expressionist school. Kurt Jooss, Trudy Schoop, Martha Graham, Doris Humphrey, José Limón and Vera Verchinina are some of the names which it calls to mind. It is rather significant to note that, with the obvious exception of the last-named artist, none of these choreographers had a severe classical training.

This may explain a certain reluctance on their part to translate every movement of the music, and every incident of the plot, into gestures of the ballet. They all stress the importance of the miming and general intellectual build-up of the dance theme, in preference to a purely musical aspect of the dance.

This does not imply that the presentations of the modern dance theatre are unmusical; on the contrary, some most interesting modern scores have been written especially for modern dance pieces, particularly in the United States. The contrast with the normal ballet procedure of collaboration lies in the fact that in the dance drama the theme is all-important, and determines the quality of the music needed to underline the action.

These dance dramas often exploit the human voice as well, not only to create the atmosphere, but to explain the plot. But this is not new. In examining the origins of classic ballet in the Courts of Europe, we perceive that at an early stage one of the greatest literary talents of that time, Cervantes, arranged ballets which included a spoken text to link the danced action together.

Not so very much later, these masques became the vogue. Real literature, however, had little to do with these charmingly naïve fairy-tales or allegorical subjects, which continued to serve as arguments for ballets right up to the nineteenth century. Even in the romantic era, when some dramatic ballets with literary merits were created, simple ballet tales remained in favour, as they could be twisted round easily to suit the requirements of the stage, and the special talents of the leading dancers.

There was always the king who ordered captured slaves to dance, with a view to falling in love with the fairest of them, and making her his queen. Village fairs were most convenient to present the local swains, trying to outdo each other in jumping contests, in order to dazzle the village maidens. Wandering gipsies were always safe and could be relied upon to furnish colourful *divertissement* material, with perhaps a muzzled bear or two thrown in for comic relief. The wonderland of ballet remained peopled with the same familiar figures, to the delight of the audience.

FAMOUS BALLET THEMES

Giselle, or The Doomed Bride, remains one of the best examples of ballet which has survived from the last century, and is as popular to-day as ever it was. Théophile Gautier read the legend of the Wilis in a book by Heinrich Heine, and he was responsible for the outline of the original plot of the ballet.

Giselle, the sprightly peasant girl, is besieged by two lovers, the gamekeeper, Hilarion, and Count Albrecht, who is disguised as a village boy. She favours the latter and is overcome by sorrow when the rivals quarrel. When Albrecht is exposed as a Count, betrothed to a Duke's daughter, Giselle becomes frenzied and her reason gives way. She falls upon the Count's sword and dies.

According to the German legend, girls who love dancing too much and die before their marriage are changed into Wilis. The gloomy setting of the second act reveals Giselle's tomb. At the command of the evil Queen of the Wilis she rises and dances for her lover, in order to lure him to his death. Giselle is not entirely under the spell. She defies the Queen, but Albrecht leaves the protection of the tomb and dances with the Wilis until he is exhausted. Daybreak comes and Giselle and the Wilis vanish, leaving the disconsolate Albrecht, cherishing nothing but a memory, lying prone upon her grave.

Though minor incidents of the plot have often been changed throughout the years, the main characteristics remain unaltered, and its grave beauty continues to stir audiences of all ages.

Artistically, *Coppelia* stands half-way between the romantic appeal of *Giselle* and the classic perfection of the Tchaikovsky ballets, *Swan Lake* and *Sleeping Beauty*. These two ballets are fairy-tales, and the dramatic action is less important than the delight of purely classical and purely musical dancing.

The libretto of *Coppelia* is based on a story by E. T. A. Hoffman and owes much of its lasting success to the plot, unfolding a *ballet d'action*, as well as to the score of Léo Délibes. It was first produced at the Paris Opera in 1870.

The fantastic theme fired the imagination of the choreographer, who took full advantage of the possibilities offered by the role of an animated doll to exploit the mechanical precision of dancing on the points.

The puppet-maker, Coppelius, is a kind of Mephistopheles, who wants the soul of the village boy, Franz, and uses a beautiful doll, which he brings to life, as a decoy. The village beau, betrothed to Swanilda, is the symbol of youth. Wavering between his love and his curiosity, he is fatally attracted by the doll's strange and mysterious beauty. Coppelius forces his doll to dance, and she inspires the passions of those who behold her, but like another Golem she unbridles forces which almost slay her own master. Swanilda, who impersonates the doll to trick Coppelius, finally recovers her bridegroom, and the lovers are reconciled, to the joy of all concerned.

The ballet theme of *Coppelia* is a perfect example of an entertaining libretto in a light vein, but with dramatic possibilities. It has lost nothing of its youth and freshness, and is a stand-by of most ballet companies to-day. Interesting detail: the role of Franz used to be danced in *travesti*, and this tradition has been kept alive in the Paris Opera, where a girl still takes this part.

In contemporary repertoire there is a leaning towards national and historical themes. The fairy-tales of Hans Andersen, used for various ballets of the Copenhagen company; and the *conquistadores* ballet, done by the Lissabon dancers, which is based on part of Camoens's epic, *Os Lusiadas*, are striking examples of this.

The symbolized history of young countries inspired such ballets as Martha Graham's *Appalachian Spring* in the United States, and Borovansky's *Terra Australis* in Australia. Further examples of national trends translated in the form of ballet are *Mr. Punch*, the ballet of Walter Gore in the repertoire of the Marie Rambert Company, and the ballets with a cowboy flavour such as Eugene Loring's *Billy the Kid*, and *Rodeo* of Agnes de Mille.

A literary ballet of our time, as far-reaching in its impact as any great novel, is Antony Tudor's *Pillar of Fire*, composed on Arthur Schoenberg's *Transfigured Night*, and created by the American Ballet Theatre in 1942. The name of Nora Kaye, the dancer who created the role of Hagar, the central figure, will remain linked with the fame of this ballet.

The time is the turn of the century, but this tragedy of a tormented soul is of all ages. It contrasts the frustration of the woman, Hagar, in the loneliness of being unloved, with the easy sensuality and coquetry of the younger sister who is able to attract the Friend, and the righteous indignation of the elder sister, prototype of a bitter spinster. Hagar's feverish imagination brings the Lovers-in-Innocence and the lowly Lovers-in-Experience to life. The reappearance of the Friend, with his promise of love and companionship, appeases finally her troubled soul.

Hagar is as moving and as real as if she were a great actress speaking inspired lines—or as if she were the neighbour's daughter whom we knew intimately. A deep surge of emotion, alternating with sudden impulses, makes this ballet theme the very essense of the dance, and at the same time curiously related to some of the great works of American literature (Steinbeck and Hemingway). It is an example of naturalism transfigured by poetry, and ideally adapted to the medium of modern ballet. It may well go down in the history of the dance as one of Antony Tudor's masterpieces of choreography.

LITERARY VALUES IN MODERN BALLET

An advantage of a romantic theme in ballet is the facility of adapting it to fairy-tales and making use of the weird and the supernatural. There is in

73. The first act of 'Giselle', by the Borovansky Ballet

74. Nina Fonaroff and Eric Hawkins in 'Appalachian Spring', Martha Graham Company

75. Martha Graham creates 'Death and Entrances', inspired by the life of the Brontë sisters

76. Antony Tudor's 'Romeo and Juliet', with Markova and Hugh Laing

77.   Period costumes in "Romeo and Juliet", with Roland Petit and Ludmilla Tcherina
in the French production

78. Antony Tudor's 'Pillar of Fire' with Nora Kaye and Tudor

79. Martha Graham in the dance poem 'Letter to the World'

the romantic style of ballet, furthermore, the *ballet blanc*, executed musically and, if well danced, entirely satisfying, without any need of intellectual approach.

A dramatic story, however, must be acceptable in every detail, and the interpretation of the individual performers must be psychologically right, to add depth and feeling to the dancing. A literary plot should attempt the portrayal of real characters in contrast to the make-belief of the romantic fairy-tales. It should appeal to the senses just as much as any romantic ballet, but in addition to this it should appeal to the intellect.

We may safely assume that only Diaghilev and his collaborators brought new ideas to the classic ballet during the first quarter of this century. Their creations, basically classic, contained all sorts of new elements. Jazz rhythms might be added *(The Cat)*, or acrobatics *(Le Train bleu)*, the subtle sophistic-ation of the slightly decadent *(Les Biches)*, the lure of the Orient *(Scheheraza-zade)*, or the primeval instincts of the dim past *(Le Sacre du Printemps)*. In spite of the intellectual approach, these outstanding ballets were essentially right, because the dance remained of supreme importance.

The further experiment was tried of adding the explanation of the spoken word to the ballet. Ida Rubinstein, who declaimed better than she danced, commissioned Paul Valéry, nestor of French poets, to write texts for at least two of her ballets. Robert Helpmann, actor as well as dancer, combined his two mediums of expression in his first important ballet, *Comus*, inspired by Milton's poem. Doris Humphrey, the expressionist choreographer of the United States, uses an essentially literary theme to compose her dance drama *Lament for Ignacio Sanchez Mejias*, after Garcia Lorca's magnificent poem. The lines are spoken and danced by one of the main figures, Destiny, and José Limón personifies the matador, as only he could.

The modern dance drama of the United States is remarkable for its literary approach to ballet themes, in which, as well as subjects of universal interest, themes of a national character are exploited. Martha Graham's *Appalachian Spring* is a good example of this style. The action depicts the early-American Mr. Everyman's wedded bliss, symbolized by the building of his house in the spring. Apart from the husbandman and his wife, there are typical village characters, led by the revivalist and his followers.

These dance dramas may be entirely convincing, but they are not ballet. One almost regrets the absence of the spoken word, which would make the significance of the rhythmic pantomime much clearer. There is always, however, a structural handling of groups, after the examples of the classic ballet as well as of the Central-European schools. Sometimes this architectural design is supremely and musically done, and puts the production on a high plane.

The weakness of other dance compositions with a literary approach lies in their ambitious claim to universal appeal. Those with a highly literary plot appeal, however, only to a small group of connoisseurs. The urgent necessity for an explanation in the programme of all the implications of the dancing seems to the balletomane a sign of weakness, because his creed is that the dance should, in the last instance, explain itself.

Literature has inspired many famous ballets of our era. A poem of Stéphane Mallarmé gave birth to Debussy's *L'Après-midi d'un Faune*, which in turn inspired Nijinsky to the creation of his choreographic poem. Fokine's *Don Juan*, Balanchine's two versions of *Orpheus*, and the various ballet versions of *Romeo and Juliet* are among a host of ballets, centring round a theme made famous in literature.

Whether one approves of it or not, the general interest in a more intellectual approach to the dance drama has come to stay. It has unmistakably taken on great importance in the post-war era. It is quite possible that for a few more years to come it will suffer from an overdose of eagerness, natural to its youth, before finding its rightful place in the realm of the dance. It has already become clear that the peasant lore of old has given way to more complicated city lore when the plot of a new ballet is being sought.

CHAPTER TWELVE

THE DANCE IN SPAIN

Truly, dancing is the very soul of beauty
Lope de Vega, The Dancing Master

THE BULL-FIGHT CONSIDERED AS A FORM OF BALLET

FOLK-DANCING in Spain has had an important influence on modern ballet, and also on the free-movement dance. Its early history is woven around mediæval Court life in Spain, and has been influenced by the dance art of the wandering gipsies, and by the Moorish domination of the country. Several regional types of dancing have their roots in far remote periods. Phoenician and Greek influences can be traced in the dance of the Catalan province. The intricate steps of the Basque dances stand out as something entirely different from any other form of folk dancing, and there is a theory that they are derived from the supposed lore of the mythical continent of Atlantis, of which the Basques claim to be the only survivors.

Dancing is extremely popular is Spain, and interwoven with the daily life of the people to a surprising extent. One form of this outpouring of their fiery temperament is the dancing of the bull-fight *(corrida)*, for in such terms the performance can be described. The *corrida* is closely akin to the sacrificial dances of old. It is a pagan rite, in which a victim is sacrificed in blood and glory. The fanatic enthusiasm it inspires in all Spaniards, young and old, male and female, amounts almost to a form of worship.

The *corrida* is not a gloomy *danse macabre*. On the contrary, it is a play of grace, gay colour, dignity, and skill. The principal dancer is the matador, and the character dancer is the bull. Incidental numbers are given by the members of the *cuadro* or bull-fighter's team. This includes three auxiliary fighters, who assist the matador in moments of danger, and in a graceful *pas de trois* they 'play' the bull with their capes. Others are the two *banderilleros*, who jump over the barrier into the arena, and swing their gaudy streamers before planting the darts in the bull's neck. The stiff figures of the two picadors with their wooden lances, mounted on their gaunt horses, form a comic relief. A gay note is added by the *monos*, or 'monkey-servants', dressed from top to toe in blood-red, who run for their lives as soon as the bull approaches.

There is dramatic suspense when the matador takes his sword in the last act and prepares for the sacrifice. With a disturbing alternation of immobility and rhythmic movement, he performs the tragic last dance of the ballet.

There is much in the art of bull-fighting to connect it with the ballet. It is an art practised in various styles, which have been evolved throughout five centuries. There is the modern school of Ronda with its stress on posturing, and daring improvisations in front of the bull. The superb length of line is accentuated by the graceful sweep of the cape.

The orthodox school of Seville, with its traditional style of passes, is more romantic in softer movements, harmoniously flowing from one into the other. The national heroes of the arena, such as Juan Belmonte and Joselito, of glorious memory, were known for their *estilo*, the purity of their line, the grace of their rotating movements, and the strength of their wrists in handling the sword. They danced their way into the hearts of their audiences just as a Pavlova did, and they are remembered with as much emotion.

Throughout the spectacle there is a continuous undercurrent of tension and excitement. There is a life at stake—and it is not always clear who will be the victim of the sacrifice, the bull-fighter or the bull. The fiercest bulls, obtained by selective breeding, are chosen from the most reputed stock farms and those which have made the bravest show in the arena are granted their lives in order that they may beget offspring.

The red blood flows. Something primitive stirs in the hearts of the masses, for this ballet is crowned by the ceremony of death. This ritual, which has its liturgies in strictly defined and stylized sequences, takes its course.

The fighter is magnificently clad in embroidered jacket and knee-breeches, and on his pigtailed head is the traditional three-cornered velvet hat. He shows off his grace and nimbleness in the precise footwork of the various passes. Here is a *veronica*: glide, turn, double pirouette, glide—the equivalent of any ballet *enchaînement*. There is a *mariposa*, which he performs in a half-turn with the cape whirling round him, and here is a *navarra*—a beautiful gesture in which the arms open like a flower, followed by a studied immobility of great dignity, and a rapid movement ending in a jump and a half-turn.

The bull-fight fan, whose technical knowledge of the rules is as great as his enthusiasm, is the twin brother of our balletomane. His thirst for æsthetic satisfaction and dramatic beauty is quenched by the bull-fight in much the same way as a balletomane's appetite is satisfied by a performance of ballet with Massine, Tchaikovsky, and Benois on the programme.

REGIONAL DANCING

Spain has a greater variety of national and regional dances than any other country, with the exception, perhaps, of Russia. In order to understand their range of style and character one must bear in mind the variegated population of the Peninsula, and the foreign influences which have swept over the country throughout the ages.

The popular idea of a Spanish dance conjures up castanets, an embroidered shawl, a flounced skirt, and gipsy exuberance. In reality the castanets are only used in special instances, the gipsy style is specific, and flounced skirts belong to Andalusian dress. Many Spanish dances, those of the North in particular, have no castanet accompaniment, and they are pastoral and gay rather than emotional and frenzied. These are the rustic dances which are difficult to adapt, and which, consequently, are seldom seen on the stage outside Spain.

The *muneira* of the Pyrenees is a gay country dance, which portrays rather comically the naïve coquetry of the village maiden. Its style is anything but 'typically Spanish'.

The *fandango* is danced in the Basque province and on the French side of the border. It is a group dance, originally performed by men only. The *pas de basque* known in ballet idiom has nothing to do with it, but the *Basque fandango* step is sometimes encountered in the Andalusian *seguidillas*. A gipsy version of this same *fandango* hails from the South and takes the form of a strong and speedy solo dance. It may be assumed that the severe climatic conditions of the North have restrained the style of its regional dancing, but inter-province exchange is apparent, particularly in the more modern stage adaptations.

The *jota* of Aragon and the *sardana* of the Catalan province are austere in line, with many intricacies of rhythm, not apparently Spanish to the uninitiated. The *sardana* of Catalonia is a group dance, of which some three hundred variations are known. Just before the outbreak of the Civil War, Maestro Mataz of the *Sociedad Catalan Sardanista* organised an artistic expedition into the mountains. In remote villages several almost extinct forms of this dance were filmed. The songs were recorded and sketches were made of the costumes.

The *sardana* orchestra consists of ten instruments, including old forms of the flute, the reed-pipe, and the bagpipes. It is said that Greek influences can be traced both in the music and in the embroideries on the costumes. The many sequences and steps of this dance vary very slightly, and when a few hundred of them are assembled the documentary material offered is a happy hunting ground for the artist, who can reconstruct at least one effective stage dance from the many suggestions offered.

The *jota* of Valencia is danced by men and women without castanets which, however, are *de rigueur* for the *jotas* of Navarre and Aragon. The real home of the castanets is Andalusia, where practically all the women's dances are accompanied by the click of castanets. In Aragon a slightly larger castanet is played with great vigour by the men and the women. The music of the castanets carries the contrast between the temperaments, male and female, far into the realm of the dance. They are played with boisterous virility by the men, and answered by the women in staccato, dry-toned, matter-of-fact rhythms. It is fascinating stuff, but it is not as moving as the castanet music of the South, where it speaks a much subtler language—a mysterious beckoning, a whispering and shouting, pride and provocation, ardent wooing and women's submission, male strength and female willingness.

Most dances of the North are executed in the local rope-soled footwear, faintly reminiscent of the ballet shoe, but naturally without the padded toe. This is in contrast with the fashion of the South, where the woman wears high-heeled shoes and the man nails iron on his heels, so that he may tap the louder and strike fire from the pavement. This clicking of the heels is absent in the North, but elevation is stressed, and the jumps of the man are curiously reminiscent of ballet.

This similarity to ballet is most striking in the Basque country, where complicated dance dramas are enacted, originally inspired by war-dances. Their remote origin is fairly obvious. The central figure may be the horse-dancer, and he 'wears' the horse as if it were a crinoline. Whip in hand, he gallops and prances around, but not in the crude way one might expect of a peasant dance. The mastery of dance technique is remarkable. It enhances the value of the group dancing.

Dr. Th. Pigeaud, in his admirable work on the Indonesian dance, mentions similar horse-dances in the centre of Java. This similarity of folk-art is puzzling but by no means an isolated case.

At one time church dancing was very popular in the North of Spain. In Saragossa Nativity dances are still performed in the church cloisters. These northern provinces honour their traditions. Then, too, there is the old religious plain-song, used to accompany the very simple children's dances of Palm Sunday and Twelfth Night. Another legacy of church dancing still survives to-day. In Seville, during Holy Week, the church minuet is danced in the Cathedral. During High Mass on Easter Sunday ten page-boys, clad in authentic seventeenth century costumes, with velvet berets and ostrich plumes, gravely perform the *Danza de los Seises* in front of the high altar.

The gipsy influences and the Moorish style, which have so obviously moulded the dance forms of the South, never invaded the North. The gipsy style of Andalusia belongs to the sphere of the *flamenco* proper, which has pervaded the folk-art of Andalusia to a point where it is difficult to define the beginning of the one and the end of the other.

Many Southern towns possess their own local dances. Ronda has the *rondena*, Valencia the *jota valenciana*, Sevilla the *sevillanas*, Malaga the *malaguenas*, etc. The Moorish-Oriental influence is frequently revealed in the positions and attitudes held by the dancers, who oppose but never touch each other. Theirs is ardent wooing, voluptuous and languorous grace, elegance of impassioned movement, with soft, feline steps. Their guttural dance songs and hand-clapping are often their only accompaniment. The music is played on the guitar, the mandoline, the gipsy tambourine, and the castanets.

The text of the song can be archaic or modern. Many dancers possess the gift of improvising their own dance songs as they go along, adroitly followed by the guitar. When the audience is well disposed it joins in the chorus. Encouragements such as '*salero, bien parada, anda la novia*', meaning 'spicy, well posed, come on, my beauty!' are shouted as marks of appreciation and encouragement. Wide-brimmed Andalusian hats are thrown onto the stage, and the dancer gracefully throws them back to their owners, with an astounding accuracy of aim.

When a folk-dance is performed on the stage by professional dancers it is generally modified, to enhance its effects and lend it a greater appeal. The *chaconne*, the *fandango*, and the *bolero* are well-known ancient dances, adapted in the nineteenth century to the romantic Spanish ballet style, which reached a peak of popularity about 1835. They were danced on the points to the accompaniment of castanets, but the traditional gestures of the arms and the upper part of the body were preserved. They represented a curious example of over-cultivated and badly adapted folk art, for which famous composers of the day wrote special music.

The conventions of the Spanish dance are strict. The *bolero* is a good example of a traditional dance form jealously preserved. It is divided into sequences. First comes the *paseo*. The dancer swaggers proudly, swinging a broad-brimmed hat and perhaps shedding a gorgeously embroidered cloak. Then comes the *diferencia* with a change of step. The next phrasing is the *traversia* with a change of place. The dance, starting from comparative immobility, is tapped out 'on the square space of a handkerchief', and is in that phase curiously reminiscent of classic Indian dancing. But it becomes slowly more extensive and more dynamic. The finale works up to a rapid climax, culminating in the *bien parada*. This is a sudden immobility, typical of many gipsy dances, and means 'well finished'. It always comes as a surprise to dancer and audience alike. The music stops abruptly, and the dancer must show consummate skill in order to achieve a harmonious pose of perfect immobility. A shaky finish is as bad as the wobbly arabesque of the ballet-dancer.

An important part of the technique is a smooth execution of *pita* and *palmada*—a beating together of the palms of the hand combined with a snapping of the fingers, and sometimes even of the finger-nails.

Rhythm and counter-rhythm are at play, interspersed with an infinite variety of heel-beats. Men and women are past-masters in the two, but the *pita* and *palmada*, only used by the women in the absence of castanets take on their full significance when done by men. They are able to cover an extensive range of expression with this finger-snapping, which seems to echo the thunder of unbridled passion which is stamped out on the floor in a crescendo of staccato heel-beats.

THE GIPSY INFLUENCE

The riddle of the mysterious origin of the gipsies has never been solved, and though the name indicates Egypt as their homeland, several racial characteristics point rather to Persia. Whether they are called *zemganos*, *roms*, *zigeuner*, or *gitanos*, they are all members of the same wandering tribe.

In Spain the musical art of the *gitanos* is called *cuadro flamenco*, as performed

81. Vicente Escudero dances 'El Garrotin', famous gypsy solodance

82. The celebrated Spanish couple Rosario and Antonio in the fiery flamenco dance 'Los Chavalillos'

83. Antonia Mercé, the celebrated La Argentina

84. Antonio de Triana teaching his daughter, Luisita, a Jota

85.   Doris Niles and Serge Leslie in Navarese Duo from Massenet's 'Le Cid'

86.   Encarnación Lopez, known as Argentinita, with Manolo Vargas in a Farruca

87.   Doris Niles in 'Alborado del Gracioso' of Ravel

88.   Australian-born Adele Romano in four movements of a Bolero Clássico

by a band of dancers and singers. This use of the word *flamenco* (meaning Flemish) is confusing. It is probable that at one time the Spaniards designated all foreigners, except their Latin neighbours and the Moors, as belonging to those far-away countries of the North, of which they knew little. The gipsy wanderers arriving from the other side of the Pyrenees were naturally called *flamencos*.

The weird, guttural monotony of the *gitano* songs stands in vivid contrast to the velvet fire and mesmeric intoxication of their dances. Their dance songs are very similar in form to the Persian mystical songs *(deblas)*. This similarity in text and tune has given rise to the supposition that these races were closely related. The gipsies, being nomads, express in the poetical though often incoherent text of their songs their revolt against social order, and their melancholy despair.

The *gitano* songs have also undeniable similarity with Jewish laments. They were at their zenith during the Moorish reign in Andalusia, and it is to be supposed that all their Oriental affinities are an inheritance from that past, which remains so strongly perceptible in their *flamenco* art.

This art has a long history. Pliny wrote of the Spanish dancers at length. The Roman matrons knew the use of castanets which they handled with elaborate elegance. Some pairs were made of ivory, or rare woods, inlaid with pearls. The dancers took as much care of them as they do to-day. To mellow their tone the castanets were worn near the dancer's body, to warm them up. Whether this really improved their tone is uncertain. It is more probable that the idea was animistic, and that the wearer hoped that some of his personality and spirit would enter the wood.

The roving fairs of the Middle Ages knew the Spaniards, who joined them as jugglers, mimes and dancers. The early rise of ballet as a stage dance forced their more unsophisticated folk-dance to take second-place, but the vogue for ballet in Spain round about 1820 helped to create the Spanish ballet style, which incorporated the folk-dance.

Cadiz and Granada were strongholds of the *gitanos*. Their *Tango Gitano* was practised a century before the Argentine *Gaucho Tango* became known in Europe. Only the names are similar. The tango of Cadiz is different in rhythm, and wholly oriental in feeling. It has the same syncopation of rhythm as the *habanera*, which had its origin in the days of Spain's colonial glory in South America. Although this *habanera* is considered to be a typical *flamenco* dance, it has definitely a creole background. It is a dance of languor, heel-clicking, fierce ecstasy and voluptuous movement. The popular *habanera* from the first act of Bizet's *Carmen* is a good example of its mood.

The *farruca* and the *fandango* are gipsified Andalusian folk-dances, which are now favourite solo numbers for men and women. The first one is typical in the virility of its heel-beats and whirlwind turns (Massine's Miller's Dance in *The Three-cornered Hat*). The *fandango* is its feminine counterpart.

Other standard dances, which to a certain extent can be improvised within their fixed outlines, are the *bulerias*, the *alegrias*, and the *garrotin*. They all belong purely to the *cuadro flamenco*, in contrast with the more sedate *sevillanas* and *seguidillas*, which are real Andalusian peasant dances, seductive in the whirl of the flounced skirt and in the rhythm of the castanets, but never as bold and abandoned as the real gipsy dances.

The inborn talent of the *gitanos* for miming is demonstrated in the sinuous movements of these dances. They move their hips, shoulders and chest simultaneously. They have no inhibitions and indulge freely in exhibitions of the grotesque. Only a few of them have taken up dancing seriously. The others, professional or amateur, prefer to perform in obscure taverns or in the open air, surrounded by their own people. They are always to be seen whenever there is a cattle-market or a fair. A dancer may cock an impudent eye at the unsuspecting foreigner and note with satisfaction that while he is enthralled by her dancing, a brother *gitano* is demonstrating his skill in the art of pickpocketing. She may even symbolize her approval in her dance.

Dancing in Spain is as natural an act as breathing. It is used on all occasions and to express all moods. The *jaleo*, a dance which is tricky on account of frequent digressions in counter rhythm, is often performed during periods of mourning. In the island of Ibiza, off the coast of Valencia, the widows are allowed, after a year of solitude, to dance in public a grave dance of dignity and restraint.

When men and women dance together there is a marked contrast between the rigidity of the male body, the rigidity of a steel spring, and the flexibility of the female in abandoned movements, but always proudly erect, head thrown backwards, chest to the fore, in the curves of the letter S. The partners dance opposite each other, but they never touch. To do so would be considered highly improper.

MODERN STAGE DANCING

Many of the great dancers of yesterday were gipsies. La Faraona and Pastora Imperio inspired Diaghilev to put on a *cuadro flamenco* as a ballet with some original native dancers, but they were not a success. Away from their own country and local atmosphere they were dumb; they missed the divine spark which could only be ignited by the frantic enthusiasm of their own public, whose mood they reflected in their dance. Only a few of them were able to discipline their wild instincts, to regulate their emotions and improve their talent by study.

Three of them, Juan Martinez, Vicente Escudero and Antonio de Triana, found their spiritual home in Paris and became famous abroad. Escudero, a friend of Pablo Picasso, remains unrivalled as a male solo dancer, but he failed in his attempt to modernise Spanish ballet.

La Argentina (Antonia Mercé) raised Spanish dancing from the level of the music hall to that of the concert platform, and put her great talent to the service of contemporary Spanish composers, whose works she made famous with her exquisite dance compositions.

She was born in the Argentine, and went to Madrid in early childhood, in order to study ballet. Though she soon abandoned classic technique, the body control and the taste for music which she acquired from it may have had something to do with her subsequent success.

Her reputation was made in Paris, and she only went back to dance in Spain when she was world famous. For ten years, until her untimely death in 1936 (she collapsed while rehearsing in front of a mirror in her villa in Biarritz), she was one of the greatest artists of the dance world.

Her mastery of castanets was complete. To hear even a record of her playing is a revelation. Her glowing personality, the charm of her wide smile, and the irresistible wit of her interpretations made each dance a delight in itself. And she showed the world, for the first time, the great variety of Spanish dance forms, and the extensive range of its moods and styles. She could transform each new creation with her inner radiance. Like a Pavlova or a Duncan in her prime she might have been a consummate exponent of any form of art she touched. She possessed the magic wand. Whatever she undertook became light, glory, and beauty unsurpassed.

Argentinita (Encarnación Lopez) was, as her name indicates, in many respects a 'little Argentina'. She had varied talents and, as well as dancing, she sang folk-songs with a deceptive and disarming naïveté. She had neither the strength nor the wit of Argentina, but a charm all her own, and a robustness which made her peasant dances very convincing. She was eclectic and her repertoire covered the entire range of regional dancing, and included, furthermore, such composed pieces as the *Sun Dance of the Incas*, or the more authentic Peruvian dances. Pilar Lopez, her partner and sister, though possessing much less culture, sometimes showed the half-forgotten gipsy abandon of her youth. She then danced as if possessed, and evoked the moon-lit nights of the Sacre Monte near Granada, when the silhouette of the Alhambra is outlined against the clear sky. She could electrify the most reserved audiences, and was greatly aided in this by Antonio de Triana, who partnered the sisters at one time.

Since her death, at the end of the war, a few Spanish dancers of pre-war fame have taken over, and there are really popular figures left. La Teresina and Laura de Santelmo, as well as Argentinita's former partner, Federico Rey (incongruously of Dutch extraction) all have a certain following.

Modern Spanish music has been weaving its spell over audiences of the concert hall. It has helped most of the modern Spanish dancers to compose their best numbers. De Falla's *Fire Dance* and the *Tango* of Albeniz are often heard, in very different dance interpretations. French composers also have been inspired by Spain, notably Debussy and Ravel.

Some foreign dancers succeed very well in the interpretation of Spanish dances. In spite of the lack of authenticity, their style may have a flavour of Andalusia, and their technique borrows attitudes and steps from the Spanish idiom.

The essentially masculine strength of this style has been shown by several outstanding modern dancers of to-day. Mention has already been made of the influence of the Spanish dance on ballet. Expressionist dancers such as Harald Kreutzberg, Alexander Sakharoff and Ted Shawn have shown conclusively that this dance medium possesses a multitude of artistic possibilities. Another dancer, whose stage name is Manuela del Rio, has made the Spanish dance her exclusive medium, whereas the more versatile Californian, Doris Niles, who possesses the advantage of a finished castanet technique, scores with poetical interpretations of the Spanish spirit such as Debussy's *Puerto del Vino*, or Ravel's magnificently Andalusian *Alborada del Gracioso*. These foreign artists are able to translate Spain as they feel it, in a very personal style, which, nevertheless, may radiate the potency of Spanish charm.

In the last few years there has been almost a surfeit of Spanish talent travelling the world, and establishing themselves firmly in public favour.

Of these Antonio and Rosario easily hold their own as public idols number one, where ever they go. Antonio, main choreographer and by far the strongest of the two, has that elusive something which marks artists of genius. Neither his lithe strength, his superb technique of castanets and ta- coneos (heelbeats), nor his dark good looks have much to do with this. It is just that something which marks great artists, whether they are superb technicians or not. Pavlova, the indefatigable worker had it, and Isadora Duncan, the erratic.

The gipsy lore of Carmen Amaya and her numerous tribe of dancing relatives comes over in a different vein. Her appeal is more primitive, more Oriental and, as far as Spanish dance art is concerned, entirely flamenco of the South. From her group came two youngsters, who by now might be considered the next best known Spanish dance couple: Teresa and Luisillo. Theirs is the monotone of the eternal love duet, infinitely stirring... but Luissillo's choreographic talent is emerging, and we may well expect some more significant ensemble works from him in times to come.

Jose Greco, Italian born one time partner of Argentinita, has also formed a company. His success is considerable, and in Spain he has done some valuable film work. All the same there seems a certain professional slickness about his work, which shows particularly in the rather poor choreography of non-authentic 'Spanish ballet', whereas some of the highlights of his programme, such as the Bolero of Ravel, done alternately in classic Spanish and true Gitano style, belong to Argentinita's memory.

Of the younger ones established in Spain, hardly seen outside their coun- try, we must yet mention Gitana Blanca and her four excellent male part- ners, and the very strong group of Pilar Lopez. The latter has in Manolo Vargas, and the young Alberto Lorca some excellent material and her repertoire though perhaps less spectacular than most, is by far the most artistic. She truly carries the great tradition in the grand manner.

CHAPTER THIRTEEN

CREATION OF A BALLET

Music, Song, and Dance: Three Apostles of Peace
Rudolf Orthwine

INITIATION

I was young, eager and ignorant. I saw Pavlova dance. I fell in love with ballet.

Though these scraps of information are entirely irrelevant, so far as a history of the dance is concerned, I have to give them in this chapter, because it deals with a ballet script I wrote myself. I want to explain how, in my particular case, the idea of a dance-story evolved. It might interest the reader in his attempt to elucidate an artist's approach to dance problems.

The Scriabin ballet, *Les Forces Errantes*, enjoyed a genuine success when it was presented in its entirety at the Théatre du Parc, Brussels, in 1939, and when excerpts from it were first given at a performance in the Salle Pleyel in Paris. It shared the fate of many dance creations—a short dream of ephemeral beauty—and then oblivion.

But it was a first child. I loved it as such, and I think that the tale of its growth might throw some illuminating side-lights on those by-paths of the theatre, to which the public is not—and never should be—admitted.

When I was a stage critic in Paris during the thirties, going to the theatre became almost a nightly routine for me, and I saw practically everything put on in the dance world, from the much-advertised nights of official ballet in the Paris Opera to the dance recitals in the concert halls. I never missed the better-class turns in the revues, nor the slightly arty and intellectual chamber ballets and solo recitals in the less commercialised little theatres, such as the Salle d'Iéna.

Visits to the studio of Alexander Volinine, who had been Pavlova's partner for ten years, and who to-day is still considered one of the best coaches for male dancers in Paris, followed. They gave me a certain basic knowledge of technique. This, though not essential to the ballet lover, should be acquired by the dance critic if he wants to speak with authority.

Gradually I became aware of the dance possibilities of certain types of music. My youthful enthusiasm carried me to the extreme of wanting to translate all the music I heard into movement, colour, and plastic rhythm.

At that period I was working on a series of articles on the Spanish dance, the outcome of a prolonged visit to Spain and of many talks with maestro José Otero, of Seville. This work brought me into contact with one of his pupils, Doris Niles, a promising young dancer from California, established in Paris. She possessed the ability of being able to interpret romantic ballet and vigorous folk-dance equally well—and she shared my love for both.

Being privileged to watch her in her studio, and to see some of her new dances taking shape after many rehearsals, the understanding of choreographic possibilities and their application in practice gradually dawned on me. The music of Scriabin, which was to be used for one of her solo dances, ignited some spark of imagination in my brain. The idea of a ballet germinated and developed.

It is true that a choreographer, when developing the idea of a new ballet, has often the peculiar qualities of a particular performer in view. When a Massine composes a new ballet, with Massine the dancer taking the leading role, it is almost impossible to get away from the idea that the plot has been shaped and built up with a view to displaying his own particular qualities to the greatest advantage.

In former times, in the pre-romantic period in particular, but also at the beginning of this century, individual virtuosity reigned supreme. Irrespective of ballet plots, solo 'dance exhibitions' were fitted in to suit the favourite of the moment. In our era the dramatic and lyrical quality of the dancer are sometimes a decisive factor in the shaping of a dance plot.

In my case it seemed inevitable, impressed and guided as I was by a particular dancing talent, that in working out my musical idea into a ballet script, the personality of Doris Niles' work should influence the outline of the leading dancer's part, and shape the romantic feeling of its character.

Doris Niles brought an element of poetry to her classic roles, and a sense of line. She conveyed the impression of elongating her movements beyond the lineal gestures of arms and legs, giving the audience a sense of space. In addition, she was extremely versatile and could switch over convincingly to the entirely different medium of the Spanish dance. In those dances she was fired by the rhythmic sensuousness of the music, and the interpreter of romantic ballet became the gipsy of fierce passion and dynamic action.

This was not done spontaneously, although one got that impression. At rehearsal I became aware of the careful study and preparation which went into the making and the rounding off of each dance. With a keen theatrical sense she carefully checked and controlled each expression. What better interpreter could one wish for one's work? Here was creative ability, experience and technique. Here was a dancer who could not only inspire a dance-score, but could also accomplish its perfect interpretation.

COLLABORATION

There seems to be a good deal of confusion in the mind of the average spectator as to who is really responsible for the first conception and main idea of a ballet. In many cases the choreographer, who arranges the steps and grouping, is not the man who writes the first script, or ballet book. This balletbook, comparable to the libretto of an opera, may be entirely original. It also may be inspired by the mode or the style of the music. Sometimes the choreographer is inspired by a story, a folk-legend, or one of the world's literary masterpieces, such as *Faust*, and *Romeo and Juliet*.

No hard and fast rules can be laid down. Often all the artists responsible work so closely together that individual ideas merge during rehearsals. When the ballet is complete the choreographer would hardly know how many of the passages of the musical score were inspired by his suggestions, or altered by them. The painter may, perhaps, have added to the work of the script-writer, in order to achieve a stronger pictorial effect. Mutual aid and under-standing—and a lot of quarreling too—may have achieved that artistic unity of the various contributing arts, which is the ideal of modern ballet.

When attempting to analyse working methods one should never generalise. For each creation, even if the same artists worked repeatedly together, the system might change. Some artists—dancers, painters and musicians—con-stantly vary their approach to their art as they ripen towards maturity; others remain unchanged, but deepen their perception with the years.

In some of the Diaghilev ballets the collaboration between all artists was very close indeed. *Le Sacre* and *Petrouchka* owed an equal debt to each one of their creators. Starting from a vague outline to which all concerned contributed details, the action, dancing, grouping, colour-schemes and music gradually emerged from the rehearsals.

89.   Australian dancer Jon Marten, of the Conyn Dance Group, in their ballet 'The Bewitched'

Doris Niles, Serge Leslie, and Eraste Touraou in the
Scriabin Ballet 'Les Forces Errantes', Brussels procuction

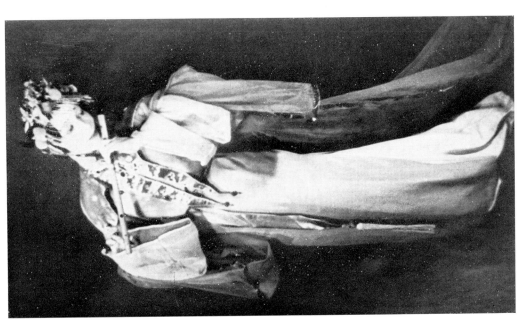

90.   Doris Niles in a Chinese character dance

91. Costume designs for this ballet by Natalie Gontcharova

92. Dance of Zulu warriors

93. Haka-Haka of Rotorua, a Maori war-dance

Masked dancer in a Javanese 'Wayang Wong' play

94. Raden Mas Boledewo in a Javanese epic ballet

95.   Principals in the Court Ballet of the Sultan of Solo (Java)

96. Masked dancers of Bali, in a Galak-type dance legend

As far as our Scriabin ballet was concerned, the composer's part was vital, because the whole conception grew out of the music. His influence, however, was necessarily a passive one, as he had died some twenty years previously. The music—as is so often the case with ballet scores—had only to be arranged, and the sequence chosen or cut down, to suit the production purposes.

Scriabin's music is of the classic-romantic type. His scores are exceedingly contrapuntal in texture, and muted brass plays a large part in the orchestral colour scheme. In his *Preludes* and *Etudes* he tried to express his idealistic mysticism. The emancipation of the human soul through ceaseless striving, and its achievement of self-expression, form the spiritual basis of his inspiration, as he himself has stated. This is never more convincingly brought out then in one of his last compositions, the *Five Preludes, Op. 74*. If ever one could express a musical mood in colour—Scriabin himself most definitely believed it possible—blue and green are the tones with which these *Preludes* should be lighted.

In the studio of Doris Niles records of some of our favourite *Preludes* were played over and over again. We talked of Scriabin's own experiments of projecting various colours on a screen in a darkened room, while playing his music. From an initial sense of colour we logically conceived shapes. The shapes took on human form and became animated with human passions. The idea of dance costumes for these still shadowy shapes followed. The ballet was born.

LES FORCES ERRANTES

This was the first outline of the ballet script: Woman, struggling against the oppression of growing darkness, is assailed by Apprehension, when the blue of the night gradually veils her green robe. This, in colour, line and rhythmic movement, expressed the mood of one of the *Preludes*, in which the serenity of the beginning is in contrast with the torment of the more agitated parts.

In the tense anxiety of the *Fourth Prelude*, the evil forces which lurk in the night of the subconscious are let loose. Music expressed the idea, the dancer expressed the music with the lines of her body, lengthened by the trailing blue mantle of night. A few amateurish costume sketches—later superbly designed by Natalie Gontcharova, of Diaghilev fame—helped my own visual imagination at that stage, to give individual shapes to the army of the Errant Forces.

The leading parts grew and became more definite in character. There was King Fever, who was to lead the entire *corps de ballet* of dark and unbridled Passions. His royal red cloak—red inevitably—threaded a line of colour through all the wavering hues of green, sulphurous yellow, blue and silver He would command his army, he would assail Woman, and spur her tormentors on to greater speed and action.

Individual characters would detach themselves from the groups. There was the Evil Tongue, of poisonous colour. Here was Ambition brightly attired. There drab Jealousy leapt forward, distorting it all and dimming the lights. Then Exhaustion, with supreme gentleness, would enfold Woman in her arms, and Sleep would triumph over King Fever's band.

Sleep, turning round and round on the points, a spinning top of silver, would induce slumber in all, and beseech the liberator, Love, to appear. The lights turn from blue to the pink of coming dawn, the dark blue of the background becomes a clear and open sky, and the Lover, the youth of all ages, is disclosed, surrounded by his followers.

There he is, wooing Sleep in a brilliant *pas de deux*, carrying her away in his arms, and wakening Woman with his touch. All the white joys of happiness accompany him. There are Caress, Tenderness and Gaiety, inducing Woman to rise and drop her weary cloak of blue and mauve.

The mazurka sweeps the last lurking shadows from the stage. The dawn of love rejuvenates Woman, who emerges triumphantly, borne high on the arms of the Lover.

A harsh *Etude* breaks into the ebbing flow of rhythm with spasmodic contortions of staccato sound. King Fever once more taints the silver light with red, and his army of poisonous colours rushes towards the tender army of Love's handmaidens, who pose on the point, hesitant but confident in their Master's victory. It is a struggle of purity against evil, of men against maids, of white against colour, of King Fever against Prince Love.

The fencing dance of Fever and Love is one of the strongest in the ballet. In the mad sweep and surge of the waves of music, Woman, too, is caught at last. In the *pas de trois* which ensues it is her own power strengthened by that of Prince Love, which finally vanquishes the dark army. When the menacing forces retreat patterns of solid colour-blocks are thrown against the sky-blue background, contrasting with the white group of Love's army.

In the final movement Exhaustion and Sleep gently lead the Prince away, and his followers, slowly moving in widening circles, disappear in their turn. Before the curtain descends, Woman, once more covered with the mauve cloak of her weariness, lies down to rest. Blue shadows creep across the stage, but they are clean and empty, and the silver light of peace radiates around her as she lies there, watched by Sleep and protected by the strength of her own heart.

This is the outline of *Les Forces Errantes*. It was performed against a back-drop of clear blue, veiled by thin curtains on which green and blue colours were projected, and which were looped back to reveal the group of Prince Love. The entire ballet was thus drenched in blue, because Doris Niles, choreographer and creator of the part of Woman, felt as much as I did myself that the musical moods were best represented that way.

An expert handling of lighting was required to suggest the subtle changes of atmosphere. The score of the electricians seemed as complicated as the piano score. The back-drop was used, as Scriabin always asked, for projecting screens to intensify with their colour the mystic effect of his melodic emotion, thus combining visual with auditory significance.

My very rough first sketches for the costumes of the principal characters were forgotten when Natalie Gontcharova, who became very Scriabin-minded herself, got the colour craze as badly as the rest of us. It was, indeed, a stroke of luck to have such a distinguished designer to collaborate with us.

As for the music, many *Preludes* were played over and over again, before the choreographer found the right sequence for the dances. Cuts were inevitable, and in several instances two *preludes* were grafted together—the first part of one, and the second part of another. Though much has been said against this cutting-up of music and this violation of the composer's original score, it often seems the only possible way in which music can be adapted for ballet purposes.

The last performance of the ballet was given just before the Germans invaded Belgium. The critics hailed Doris Niles for the poetic quality of her dancing, and for the musical strength of the choreography. Some of them mentioned the impression of complete unity of all the composite parts of the ballet. This to me was the most encouraging thing they could have said.

AUSTRALIAN VENTURE

After the war I settled in Australia. I arrived at a time when the ever-growing popularity of ballet was only just starting to touch the Australian scene. There was only one large professional ballet company, under the trustworthy direction of Edouard Borovansky, who brought all the tradition of his Russian schooling, and his experience of years with the *Ballets Russes*, to bear on his dancers. The country was hungry for culture, and eager to learn more about this strange art of ballet, of which it had only intermittently seen something, when touring companies arrived from overseas.

I started to write articles on the dance for the more enlightened magazines and collected material for this book, which was first published in Sydney in 1948 in a somewhat abbreviated version. The directors of Australia's national radio network wanted a few talks on this 'new' subject, and several universities followed suit, even organising short series of evening talks for me on the cultural development of the dance through the ages.

Interest grew allround, culminating in the establishment of a second company of classic ballet, state-subsidised, in the city of Melbourne. But ballet could only be shown in the larger towns, because of the peculiar topography of Australia, which has a sparse population equally divided between a few overgrown cities and the vast inland, where villages are few and far between.

The admirable Arts Council of Australia, working on the same lines as the British Council for encouragement of the arts, tried to remedy this state of affairs by giving subsidies to artists touring the island.

As far as I was concerned the obvious solution would have been to take the plane by myself, and give talks on the ballet to small but eager audiences, living at great distances from each other and gathering in often inadequate halls.

This, however, seemed rather a dry and academic initiation in the glorious art of the dance, which should after all explain in simple movements what it would take me hours to describe.

The answer was found in taking some pupils from the various ballet-schools which had been started in the capitals, and form them myself to take with me on tour.

I was most fortunate in finding as leading dancers two young Australians who made an ideal team: Jon Marten and Ann Challinor. They both possessed the typical Australian qualities of musicality, enthusiasm, and physical stamina. They were quick in the uptake, and with the amazing unself-consciousness of a young race they seemed to take to the stage quite naturally. They never lost their heads, were quick to improvise if need be, and in general they were just suited for the type of work I wanted of them: pioneering in the outback, and bringing ballet to the bush.

My idea was to give a lecture-recital, which we called 'The Story of the Dance' in which the uninitiated would get an idea of the development of the dance, from folkdance to ballet, passing through Court dances and national forms, such as the Spanish dance. I had chosen Jon Marten specially with this in mind, as he had started a dancing career with a teacher in Sevilla. The war had interrupted his schooling, and he had spend those years in the Navy.

For the purely classic dances, which of course could not be missed in such a survey, I secured the services of an Australian ballerina, Helene Ffrance, who had just returned from London, where she had danced with the British companies, and also in the film 'The Red Shoes'.

With the pianist we were five people. Our props consisted mostly of a few clothes baskets and a plain backdrop... consequently we were a mobile unit, which could easily be moved by plane or, for the shorter distances, by car. For touring in the more closely settled districts we sometimes had two cars, a chauffeur-stage-manager and a dresser, this miniature company could also move easily and give two performances daily and still have time left to travel in the morning and set up again in the next village, in time for perhaps an evening's performance.

Everywhere local committees, having done the spade work of organising, received us. In some instances the small hotels weren't considered comfortable enough and we would be housed privately with committee members. Our first concern would be the hall, the state of the stagefloor, the condition of the piano—sometimes sadly the worse for the weekly boogie–woogie sessions—, and the possibilities of dressing-rooms. In this vast country one sometimes needed a fire in the hall, and then again the tropical heat might be suffocating. Often we proudly took possession of a well-equipped but neglected old-fashioned theatre where, since the event of the talking pictures, no live show of professional standard had been held for twenty years. In those cases we felt our pioneering really worth while, particularly as almost everywhere the response was enthusiastic.

There were always volunteers to help improvise an improved stage lighting. If the floor was uneven, and threatened the *pointes* of the dancers a carpenter would immediately try and remedy the worst spots. When old-fashioned high footlights masked the feet of the dancers everything was done to try and improve those too. It was a normal occurrence to have the piano tuned at the last minute, or even exchanged for a less impossible privately owned one. The whole village would cooperate... even to the extent of a welcome theatre supper afterwards, where artists and public could meet each other, and answer the inevitable questions. Up till the last minute of curtain rise everyone worked hard. And then, with the last floral decoration moved to a less conspicuous spot off-stage, and the last hole in an improvised flat pinned together, the footlights would go on. One could feel the tension of an expectant full house... then our pianist would play the National Anthem, and when everyone was seated again the curtain would rise on our '*Story of the Dance*'.

To illustrate the beginning of stage dancing and ballet, as growing out of the simple, natural and spontaneous folkdances, Jon Marten and Ann Challinor would open with an old, reconstructed, Portugese folkdance, in the gay and authentic costumes. Then the ballerina would demonstrate in a more sophisticated Polish dance how already, even among the peasants, the simple dances took on depth and meaning when handed over from generation to generation.

One of my brief explanations to show the refining element of mediæval Court dancing, and the slow perfection of elementary technique of the five positions of ballet would follow. This gave the dancers time to change and to appear again: Ann Challinor or Helene Ffrance to demonstrate the positions and some other basic steps, such as the pas de chat, the relevé, échappé, ronde de jambes, arabesques, and the possibilities of elevation. These would then be linked together in an 'enchaînement', a sort of little improvised dance in which all these steps would be used.

Jon Marten then furnished the next link in the chain by reconstructing a XVIIth century Court dance, a *Gaillarde*. Then the ballerina again, on the *pointes*, dancing one of the great soli of the classic repertoire; and the couple to add some dances of humour or pathos in a more modern vein to show that the ballet need not only be solemn poetry of movement, but can be sparkling, witty and even mischievous too.

A few stage dances of national flavour would also be given, of which the authentic Spanish ones of Marten alternated with a castanet solo, or a recitation of one of the gipsy dance 'coplas'. These are the often improvised dance songs of Andalusia, in which the rhythms change, to vary the dances which are executed on this accompaniment, with the exclusion of any instruments. These items, which are rather novel to find in a dance recital, have also interested European audiences greatly. With my explanations of choreography: how to make a ballet; and some stage adaptations of a Mexican tango, a naughty French Polka (which was always encored, this being the final number in which Marten and Challinor could expel their remaining breath), and some more dramatic dances in a Central-European vein, the programme was completed.

It certainly gave those, who had never seen ballet before, some idea of the many possibilities of the dance as a complete theatrical art. And it helped to overcome some of the prevalent prejudice against the ballet in general, and male dancing in particular with very mixed audiences, in which there would be miners and sheepshearers, as well as doctors and housewives. Time and again the dancers were paid a very high tribute. They were thanked most sincerely, not only because they had entertained all these people for a single evening... but because they had given them something to think about, a new insight in a world of rhythms and harmony and beauty.

The children would be more demonstrative and exuberant, during the special school matinees organised for us. But here the same applied: we felt we were sowing a seed and building up more discriminating audiences for the future. Without a little idealism no venture can succeed. Ours is on a professional basis, commercially exploited. But the core exists, and that is why all of us, concerned in this most recent venture of 'The Story of the Dance', are happy to continue with it. We may occasionally grumble at low fees, early-morning trains, bad stage floors, untuned pianos... but when the footlights go up, and we hear the eager voices of children, looking with bright eyes towards the magic curtain, all is well. For all those who live for the theatre, there will never be a more beautiful sound than the creaking of the ropes, when the stage-manager signals: 'Curtain up'.

CHAPTER FOURTEEN

EPILOGUE:
FROM TRIBAL DANCE TO BALLET BLANC

The Dance is at the beginning and at the end of all art
Havelock Ellis

DARK AFRICA

RHYTHM is Life.

Recognition of cosmic rhythm is evident when the dance plays a dominant part in religious ceremonies. Magical incantations and the hypnotism of the spinning movements bring on a state of trance, and the knowledge that through rhythmic mesmerism a higher state of consciousness can be reached. All this is older than our civilization. The yogi mystics and the dancing dervishes, Miriam the Priestess, and the incense-drunk Delphic Oracle—they all knew the secret inherited by the African tribes.

The tomtom is subdued, but the heart-beat of its constant rhythm insinuates itself into the bloodstream. There are the warriors, splendidly nude, their height grotesquely emphasized by feathered head-dresses. Their dark muscular bodies are a contrast to the whiteness of the striped decorations painted on their oily skins.

The mystery of the murky shadows retreats when the logs burn high. Behind the shadows a deeper blackness of compact humanity lurks. Its pungent smell, intermingled with the fetid odours of the night, and the scent of aromatic wood burning, is heady like incense.

Slowly the dance begins. Movements follow the beats of the drums. The drums are talking triumphantly, in thunderous voices, answering each other. Fire, rhythm, bodies, night, burning logs, lurking shadows—and the sinister laugh of the jackal in the distance.

This is the holiest dance of all, the symbol of procreation, of man's godlike creative power. The drum's force is behind each jump and each rotating movement. The body is a mere instrument, following blindly and automatically. The high impetus of sound drives it on, and lashes it to a fury of surging passion, ardent anticipation, growing frenzy and spasmodic jerks. The drum and the man, together in rhythm, together in violence, until the tension becomes unbearable. On and on, with nerves taut. Faster still, a spinning, a jumping—the dark body is painted against the roof of the night—a climax so sudden, a silence so sudden, that for one breathless moment it seems as of the end of all things has come.

Collapse, and the overflowing silence is broken by the chattering of a monkey—or was it a child crying? Inexorably the drum starts its weird throbbing again. Nerves quiver, and the silence is as compact as the darkness broken by the flashes of sound, just as the night is slashed by flashes of lightning. The night, once more, is black with the dance of Africa.

THE MAORI 'HAKA-HAKA'

Fresh winds from the mountains whip across the blue sky. This blue of New Zealand is clear and joyous, not the menacing blue of the tropics. The golden-skinned men and women gather for the *haka tapahari*, the savage war-dance of the Maoris. To its fierceness the women lend their softer appeal. Their smile is sweet. The roundness of their dusky features is lit suddenly by the liquid flame of their eyes. But the harsh strength of the martial dance remains.

The costumes, colourful as all things Polynesian, are severe in line. The reed skirts, in slender stripes of black and white, fall straight down to the ankles, and loincloths of woven hemp are gaudily decorated. The women in front, the darker, heavy-muscled men behind, they sway and gesticulate to the chanting melody of the war song. The men jump magnificently, and their elbow movements are angular. Their heads roll, their eyes protrude, their tongues stick out in the approved heroic fashion, and their rhythm crashes through the evenly flowing tranquillity of the women's lines, as they move their feet and swing two small balls of flax *(poi)*, hanging at the end of strings, and manipulated with quick wrist movements. There is a soft, padding accompaniment of ghostly sound, when the spinning balls hit the skin, the wrists, the elbows or the knees of the dancers. And softly they sing.

Hear them sing their dance-songs, the tribal songs of former days, which exhort a dying race to take pride in their past and make a firm stand against an uncertain future:

Kamate, kamate. Kaora, kaora.
Death to the enemy. Life to us.
Here is the hairy white man,
We thought he brought us sunlight.
Be strong. O, ye faithful, be strong.
He brought us darkness. . . .

POLYNESIAN RHYTHMS

They move languorously, the girls of the South Sea Islands. A flaming crown of hibiscus flowers encircles the black hair, and the Asiatic eyes turn upwards, with wide lips dreaming. Dreams of hot nights, the oppressive silence of the mangrove forests, the sound of the surf, and the soft, yielding sand. They curve generously under the rustling straw of their skirts, and their bare feet slur along the boards. Little swishing sounds remind one of the sea, and of palm-leaves rustling in the wind. The gestures of the hand are beautiful, like pale serpents writhing, rhythm rippling from finger-tips to flat heels—bare feet—brown bodies—brown earth.

The rigidity of the male body is like steel wire. The muscles quiver in staccato movement. A man clasps a small native guitar between his knees, and beats a rapid movement, which rushes on to a climax. The women, four in a row, dance on and on, and there is the Princess with the golden hands, a fragile statue of the winds, and the two stately handmaidens, mature and sensuous, and the older woman, all hips, eyes, and hungry mouth. There is a cruel fascination in the detachment of these bodies, from which the souls are debarred. They are inhabited by rhythm, to the exclusion of all other things.

The men, stronger and more brutal, with a less remote remembrance of the animal kingdom, are dangerously alive. Unpredictable force is in them, and their eyes are aglow. They are the slayers, the killers. They will rape for the lust of violation, and will glory in their delight. All that is in their dance.

The incantation of the guitar is hypnotic in its repeated monotony. Its flow of melody cannot be stemmed. The spectator feels how the obsession of this flowing rhythm gradually masters his senses, and how it creeps under his own skin, and tugs at the bonds of his civilized restraint. Rhythm beats at the ancient walls of his inhibitions.

Suddenly it is all over. The music stops, and the spell is broken. The dancers kneel down, exhausted. The conventional round of applause is like a slap in the face of growing hysteria. All of a sudden the flaming world is humdrum once more. Frangipani blossom drifts down like snow. The *hula-hula* is finished.

THE ROYAL BALLET OF JAVA

The *Kraton* of Souracarta is the forbidden city of one of the two Sultans of Java. It lies in the centre of the island, little disturbed by the march of history. The Royal palace is the centre of the *Kraton*. The open hall *(pendopo)*, were the ballet performs, is in the centre of the palace. The sultan sits on his throne, on a dais, in the centre of the hall.

The tradition of ballet as a private Royal entertainment is ancient. In the East it has survived to this day in Cambodia, in Bali, and in Java, perhaps because of the popular belief in the king's divine descent. The ballet is his, and consequently the dancer's position has an almost religious significance. The subject-matter of the ballets is mainly religious too.

Dance themes are legendary, mythical and historical. They are taken from the classic Hindu epics, Rhamajana and Mahabharata. The manner of interpreting these is rigidly conventional in Djocjacarta, and more lenient at the nearby Court of Souracarta (also called Solo). In India, in Java and in Bali, everywhere, in fact, where the Hindu religion is practised, these dances are fundamentally the same, even if their stylized execution varies greatly with the country.

The dancing is full of symbol, expressed in the *mudras*, the language of gestures and hand positions, which is less extensive in the Javanese ballet than in the Indian dances. The slender fingers and pliable wrists of the dancers rotate and move sinuously, and each position and attitude has a meaning. The constant flow of music from the bronze-voiced *gamelang* orchestra is potent in the limbs when, with eyes downcast, the gold-clad statues glide past each other, weaving intricate group patterns, through which the solo dancers tread their way. The men dancers, golden statues too, and as gorgeously attired, pose with golden bow and arrow, or with the slender slip of the sarong tilted upwards, like a brilliant bird's tail.

The music has a mighty, metallic voice. The *gamelang* orchestra, which varies in size, sometimes contains as many as thirty men and boys, who squat in front of their instruments. The suspended gongs, of different sizes and tones, are dexterously played. When their sonorous voices boom in unison across the hall, the atmosphere of a religious ceremony is created.

The favourite dancers, pale and slender flowers of unfolding womanhood, are shadowed by the smaller ones, boys and girls, who from tender youth take their place in the ballet school, and undergo a long and severe training, before they are allowed to appear before their Sultan.

They dance—and their repetition of movement seems to us, the uninitiated, to be monotonous. The end of a batik scarf is held and flipped away in worship of the hero, Ardjuno, son of the gods. The solemn preparation for virginal sacrifice to Subadra, Ardjuno's beloved one, takes place and the long dance of chaste wooing, when expressed with symbolical and totally restrained gestures, is superbly artificial.

There is no sense of time. This ballet may go on and on, well into the morning. The song of the *gamelang* makes ripples on the surface of the night, and the dancing continues, endless and monotonous like the sea.

TRANCE DANCING IN BALI

The moon is full. The holy banyan tree spreads its aerial roots as a dark background to the sculptured beauty of the offering-house. Many people have gathered in the temple square, because two virgins are to be initiated to the temple dancing to-night. There is a glare of torches, the salt tang of the sea, and the noise of a crowd. The priest and the priestess guard the two girls in a secluded spot. They have been clothed magnificently, and are entirely swathed in hand-painted robes. Their little heads are like top-heavy, drooping blossoms, adorned by the gilded glory of cardboard crowns.

The priest and the old woman carry on a hypnotizing singsong. The girls are held over fuming incense pots. With eyes closed they sway slightly and inhale deeply. They are far away already.

The orchestra squats in a circle in the middle of the square. There are the bronze *gamelang*, and also the reed *anklung instruments*. The frail little dancers, weighed down by the heaviness of their embroideries and jewels, squat, and the priest continues his prayers and incantations.

Now the music starts, and the two *legongs*, with eyes closed, are helped to their feet. All eyes are focused on them, but they are oblivious. They are immobile. The rhythmical throb of the gongs seems to propel them suddenly into the middle of the circle, with a dramatic intensity of movement. Fans flutter and slender wrists coil. They move in perfect co-ordination of plastic movement, and with utter precision. And still their eyes are closed.

It is weird and almost gruesome to see them. It goes on and on. Time has come to a stop. It is lovely and exciting. The crystalline and flute-like chant of a boys' choir adds the last touch to this enchantment of sharp moonlight, veiled by shadows of midnight blue.

The older *legongs*, who have been meticulously trained, are adepts in the difficult technique required for these stylized movements of head, arms, fingers, and feet. Yet these children have the same degree of artistry, perhaps even more mature and finished, and they mirror each other's gestures with eerie precision.

The question is—do they really dance in dream state, without any preliminary training? It must be so. There must be atavistic influences at play. Generations of this traditional art lie behind them. They must be under a hypnotic spell. The eyes of the priest and priestess never leave them. What subtle connection is there between the will-power of those people and the execution of the finished dance by these children of ten?

There are strange, shrieking noises in the temple courtyard. Animals are being slaughtered. The cheeks of the little girls, who now squat in a state of coma, are touched with fresh blood. New strength is instilled into them. And the dance starts once more...

The moon is veiled by clouds. The rhythmical throbbing of the drums and gongs haunts our retreat. Bali retains its mysteries, of which white men may have only a glimpse—a glimpse of beauty, touched by the weird and the supernatural.

CUADRO FLAMENCO

The pale sherry wine, heady and very dry, is poured out into small glasses. The drabness of peeling walls is clouded over with a mist of cigar smoke. Round the platform an excited audience of dance lovers, mostly men, has gathered.

The *cuadro flamenco* has formed up on the rickety stage. Two of the four dancers are young and gaudily beautiful. The guitarist strums softly on his instrument, oblivious of his surroundings. The man dancer, lithe and graceful, scowls. His long face is copied from an El Greco painting. The women wear the multicoloured flounced dresses of the gipsies, with the trains *(colas)* coiling like serpents round their legs. When dancing they handle these with superb unconcern.

There is a current of sympathy between the dancers and the audience, which is essential to the atmosphere of the *flamenco*. The tension grows as the guitarist awakens from his melodic trance, and a rhythmical hand-clapping marks the rising of the first dancer from her chair.

She takes the floor alone. The others remain seated and form a background around her. They shout encouraging words. This *zapateado* is a dance of heel-beats, and is often done by men only. But la Pipiola, of local fame, has authority enough to adapt her own inventions to the conventional dance rhythms. Slowly, very slowly, she starts to beat out a provocation. The man has not yet joined her. He remains motionless, but rhythm already possesses him, and his eyes are ablaze. She turns, she moves with the voluptuous S position so typical of Spanish dancing. She clasps her slender hands, and the men, all the men in the audience, respond to her allure. Her partner, still immobile with hand on hip, awaits his cue.

A crescendo of guitar music brings a response of rapid turning. Now the hand of the man moves. He snaps his fingers softly. He is nothing but rhythm and counter-rhythm, tapping heels and clicking fingers. But he does not yet glide across the stage. He is 'dancing on the space of a handkerchief'.

Now the woman answers in the same tongue. Faster and louder, without moving from the spot, they reach an ecstasy of rhythm, and shake with an intense passion. The *cola*, a serpent of spotted white, quivers and lashes the nervous limbs. The bodies are proudly erect. The girl's head is thrown back as if in defiance, and an unholy fire burns in the man's eyes. The vibrations of the guitar become an obsession. The audience is transfigured, and adds to this weird tension of suppressed passion. They are possessed by the dance — and when the guitar suddenly stops the storm of applause is deafening. Hats are thrown on to the stage, as if it were a bull-fight, and hoarse cries of '*Olle!*' and *Salero!* are heard. The pale golden *manzanilla* flows again freely in the small glasses.

It is crude and somehow distressing. It is the truly native dance of a country where dancing has a long tradition.

METROPOLITAN INTERLUDE

The intelligentsia meets the arty crowd in the lofty studio of an important house in an important city. Sophistication is a cloak for vacuity and boredom. Society mingles with Bohemia and the press. The stage is cleared. Indradev

Prasad, the Indian temple dancer, will appear for the first time. The audience is satiated with rumba, caviar sandwiches, and the latest scandals. Their jaded palates need stronger meat.

The *décor* is a simple arrangement of dark velvet curtains and blue spot-lights. A gong sounds. The thin tune of an Oriental *rhaga* is played on the piano. A *tabla* player beats on the drum with his long, tapering fingers.

A young god appears. He is Buddha, veiled with gold. One feels he is of the first period of earthly incarnation, and the gold mark of the Brahmin caste is painted between his eyes. On breast and arms gold ornaments reflect fleeting glimmers of light. The dance of Invocation is translated in *mudras*. We, who do not speak this language, are strangely moved, although we do not understand. The grave harmony of inner rhythm, when expressed to perfection, has a universal meaning.

This dancing belongs to another world of purer simplicity, even though each gesture is inspired by a tradition a thousand years old. There is com-plete subjection of personality to rhythm and it is done with complete accept-ance of ritualistic dominion. Each gesture flows into the next, or pauses for a moment, suggesting a faintly familiar attitude.

Inspiration is an inadequate word with which to attempt a description. If in these dances religion is made visible, they are not meaningless rites, but the spirit of esoteric acceptance. Religion has been purged of the sensual and strives to attain, through the medium of the dance, a higher plane of understanding. The infinite repetitions and variations of minute detail are too subtle for our Western impatience. But the simplicity of its beauty is like a challenge flung to our occidental superiority complex. The elation, and the dawning of a new conception of the meaning of art remain, when one slips back into the routine of rye whisky and rumba.

BALLROOM DANCING

Society dances, from Court minuets to peasant polkas adapted to the ball-room, are all the same thing. A *Sir Roger de Coverley* or a *Paul Jones*, the plantation farm-dance and the waltzes of Old Vienna in the beer-gardens —they were all means to the same end. They satisfy the craving for rhythm.

The polite family balls of Victorian days, where marriageable daughters were brought out in low-cut dresses, and paraded before eligible bachelors during *lancers* and *polonaise*, and the tribal dances of the marriageable virgins of Africa, were in principle quite the same.

The matchise and the tango were polite adaptations of gaucho dances from the gambling dens of South America. They were followed by the rumba of negro origin and by a palais glide and a jitterbug heebee-jeebee. They are all passing fancies of a jazzing age, which moves between periods of pre-war and post-war crisis and unrest. An atomic age, expressing its agitation and apprehension in jitterbugging, or settling down to more folksy square dancing...

There remain the more sedate dances of the little people, the lore of harbour and factory, of market and workshop. There is the *java* of the Parisian *apache*, also danced by working girls at the Saturday night balls of the *faubourgs*. There is the *fado* of Lisbon, dear to the heart of the children of the people. Hear the complaint of the soft-voiced Portuguese girl as she sings her dance song, sentimental and brave, the old, old story of love unrequited and of hope eternal, the same story which the crooner sighs in front of the microphone when he sings a slow English waltz or a melancholy *blues*.

And the dance goes on...

AU REVOIR TO BALLET

The theatre is aflame with light. Queues have formed outside, hours before-hand. The romantic ballet will be revived to-night. Karsavina will dance *Swan Lake*. Pavlova will die superbly in *Giselle*. Nijinsky will leap to the sky in *Le Spectre de la Rose*.

Shadows of the past are deepening. The phantom grace of Marie Taglioni illuminates the stage. Fanny Elssler, voluptuous and beautiful, flits past. Carlotta Grisi poses on the point.

The lights in the house are lowered. There is a hush. The conductor raises his baton. Music, soft and enchanting, steals over the scene. There is that one intolerable moment of suspense just before the curtain rises. We are in the fairyland of *ballet blanc*...

INDEX

NOTE: The numerals in italic type indicate the plate numbers of the illustrations.

INDEX OF BALLETS

Note: The numerals in italic type indicate the plate numbers of the illustrations.